Comments:

"It is brave of you, as a clergyman, to speak out like this. It is especially important for 'insiders' to the faith to testify to its problems."
—Elizabeth Anderson, Arthur F. Thurnau Professor and John Dewey Distinguished University Professor of Philosophy and Women's Studies University of Michigan, Ann Arbor.

"Plato's 'Allegory of the Cave' tells of people who have lived their lives chained inside a cave, facing a blank wall. The only 'things' they have ever seen are shadows cast upon the wall by things passing in front of a fire somewhere behind them. A prisoner escapes to the outside world and discovers that the shadow world he had known is an illusion. Socrates tells him he must return to the cave to share his knowledge with the prisoners still at the wall.

Francis Terrene, a clergyman ... and a devoted Christian for 51 years, has escaped the cave of Christianity and has awakened to a world of wonder—the real world. Now, with no prompting from any Socrates, he returns to the cave to share his discoveries with those who still know only the shadow-world of faith. Perhaps more importantly, however, he also explains to those outside the cave the questionable means by which the shadows still are being projected on the wall, the motives of the agents running the shadow projectors, and why secularism must replace supernatural religion.

—Frank R. Zindler, Editor, American Atheist Press

"Terrene, a former clergyman himself and thus an observer from the inside, wastes no words in recounting the various indignities, horrors, or absurdities of this institution, which has had and continues to have so much presence in and influence on the social world."

—Jan Narveson, Distinguished Professor Emeritus, Philosophy Department, University of Waterloo; Order of Canada 2003.

"What makes this book special is the personal and insightful perspective that Terrene brings into his writing. It is the result of Terrene being a core part of the church for many years before becoming an atheist."

—Zoltan Istvan, *National Geographic* and *New York Times* former correspondent, and author of the bestselling *The Transhumanist Wager*.

"*Church Myths* is a passionate exposé on the damaging nature of religion. For author Francis Terrene—a former clergyman and theologian—it is clearly a cathartic narrative as well. From beginning to end, Terrene rails against the outrageous deceptions and hypocrisy of the church—often with razor-sharp wit .... He also illuminates the many nonsensical ways that various denominations brand themselves, market their products, and psychologically manipulate their followers. If you're looking for a no-holds-barred critique of religion in general and Christianity in particular, this book fits the bill.

—John Winsor, award-winning composer and author of *What Your Preacher Didn't Tell You.*

Recommended Sites:

Film Library
Center for Inquiry
Richard Dawkins Foundation

Resource Sites
Richard Dawkins
Freedom From Religion
Center For Inquiry
The Secular Web

Associations
American Atheist
American Humanist Association
Council for Secular Humanism:

Social Support Groups
Atheist Republic
Sunday Assembly
Secular Student Alliance
The Clergy Project:

Secular Alternative to Religion
The School of Life

International Umbrella
Atheist Alliance International
Secular Coalition for America
IBKA

Dedicated to:
My dear J.K. that he may be free from the fetters of religious myths;
See that the world is indeed much larger than a church enclave;
And live a creative and utilitarian life ...

Church Myths:
An insider's exposé of church exploitations!

Church Myths:
An insider's exposé of church exploitations!

Francis Terrene

*be*yond
2014

Church Myths: An insider's exposé of church exploitation. Copyright © 2014 by Francis Terrene. Published by *be*yond. All rights reserved. No part of this publication may be reproduced, distributed, or transmitted in any form or by any means, or stored in a database or retrieval system, without prior written permission from the author.

Cover photo credits: Fire & Brimstone, ID 55919© Caraman|Dreamstime.com; Freedom education logo, ID 35428165 ©Dharshani.k|Dreamstime.com. Book interior credit: Abstract People Logos, ID 5743302© Lightvision|Dreamstime.com.

ISBN: 978-0-9919259-3-3

Contents

Introduction
- 14   Why this Book?

Hallowed Trade, Commerce, and Politics
1. 18   Exclusive Claims of God and Heaven
2. 39   Franchising the Hereafter
3. 55   The Notion of Sin and the Manipulation of Conscience
4. 72   The Exploitation of Conscience
5. 87   Tithes, Offerings, and Financial Exploitation
6. 101   Holy Clergy and their Sacrilegious Affairs
7. 109   God's Will and the Despicable Agenda
8. 117   The Sense of Sacredness and the Ambience of Fear

Worldly Conquest
9. 133   Faith and the Depraved Passion

| 10. | 146 | Evangelism and Cultural Imperialism |

Fairy Tales

11.	155	Doctrinal Integrity
12.	171	The Bible and its Holiness
13.	184	The Earthliness of the Bible
14.	194	Heaven and the Primitive Worldview
15.	202	God, Patriarchs, and Myths
16.	213	Jesus Christ and Other Gods
17.	227	New Birth and Hallucination

Making Sense Out of It All

18.	243	Why the Doggedness of Faith?
19.	259	Candid Soul Searching
20.	269	Thinking Through
21.	278	Considerations Before Leaving the Church
22.	291	Why People Are Leaving the Church
23.	305	How Believers Become Atheists
24.	313	Church Transformation Needed
25.	326	Comparative Myths:

Christian and Others

Why Secularism?

26.	340	The Psyche of Believers
27.	355	Why We Need Alternative Secular Values
28.	375	The Prospects of a New "Faith"
29.	387	The Ten Principles

Epilogue

392　　En Route to a Fresh Outlook in Human Life

Endnotes

394

Introduction
Why this Book?

I've been wanting to write this book for some time now, because it touches the very core of Christian faith. Now I believe the time has come to reveal my life-changing discoveries and realizations about Christianity.

But who am I to write this revealing book about the church? *First*, I'm a theologian. *Second*, I'm a clergyman. *Third*, my journey of faith has brought me to the inner sanctum of the church. So I deeply know, firsthand, what church members, clergies, and scholars have hidden behind their facades.

I committed and sacrificed my life to the church for quite a time. Only to end up broken deep inside! I cherished the promise of Heaven and the care of God every day since my childhood. Only to end up delusional! Why? Was it about the church? Or was it about God?

I'm not writing this book as a disgruntled member of the church. But as a human being, deeply longing to share my realization about the most enslaving, yet the most adored, of the institutions our civilization has created. This book is not about scholarly research, which as a theologian I used to do. This is about candor and common sense. Not like the petty theological books written by ivory-tower theologians—preoccupied with fancy words about their fancy world.

This book was born out of my years of real life contemplations. Written as a candid revelation—with the hope that we may be free from the enslavement of religious myth. And become more creative and constructive human beings.

Hallowed Trade, Commerce, and Politics

1
Exclusive Claims of God and Heaven

If God is universal, and paradise is for all people, why does Christianity claim as the only reliable religion that will ensure humanity's access to God and the assurance of Heaven? If Jesus is a universal God, why do churches, each with conflicting sectarian doctrines, vie for sole domain of Jesus and his promised paradise?

And who really is the God Christians believe him to be? What actually is the paradise they pin their hopes on? And what truthfully is the church they regard as the ark of salvation? It's a common knowledge that the God Christians worship is Jesus. But what most people don't know, was the Jesus hidden behind the facade of Christianity.

Christians today, impulsively believed that Jesus was God incarnated. For them, proof of his divinity came from the miracles he did, such as turning water into wine, and raising the dead. His followers claimed he resurrected himself after being crucified. Then ascended to Heaven. Because of these notions, Christians assumed Jesus was the God! The one who could save them from their sins and Hell. And able to reward his believers with life eternal. Not knowing the fact, that the now common belief on Jesus' divinity—merely originated as a mandate of the council of Nicea in 325 CE.

But who Jesus really was? He was one of daring Jewish Messianic aspirants who launched his popularity by turning water into wine in a village wedding. While gathering followers, he taught pro-common people values that were non-violent and non-political. Religion in Jesus' time was elitist. Religious interpretation and teaching were reserved for an elite class in the religious bureaucracy. Although fathers could teach religion at home, but for an ordinary person to teach religion in public was revolutionary. It was both a public expression of spiritual discontentment and a protest against state-sanctioned religious institution.

Like his cousin John, Jesus wanted to start an independent ministry, detached from the controls and confinements of the state religious bureaucracy. Jesus' focus was on a personal value-driven way of life, instead of an institutionally-enforced lifestyle. He condemned the hypocrisy and financial exploitation of the temple. He abhorred the temple being turned from a quiet place for personal meditation, to a place of trade and commerce. Religion, as an institutionally regulated way of life, did not really fit well with Jesus' mindset.

Also, Jesus wasn't ascetic. Despite taking breaks from the humdrums of everyday life, he lived with the common people, and was one of them. And like any Jewish man of his day, marriage for him was sacred. In fact, in Judaism, being human is complete only in the union of a man and a woman. Judaism detested celibacy, as did the Romans and the Greeks. Family was, as it remains today, highly valued among Jews. So it was very probable that Jesus was a married man. And, as consented in ancient Judaism, he might even have had more than one wife.

The Roman Catholic Church's insistence on celibacy—an influence of the Desert Fathers in the history of the Catholic Church, expunged the consideration of Jesus as a married Jewish man. So now Christians assume Jesus was celibate. As a celibate, instead of drawing followers from among the common working people, he might have annoyed them instead. In that case, his followers might have been limited to fellow hermits. It's ironic, because while the Torah, the Hebrew scripture Jesus regarded as holy, sanctified marriage and sex, even from the very beginning of universal existence; Christians, deluded by celibate hermits, think of a married and sexual Jesus as sacrilegious.

Furthermore, if we decipher the Gospel narratives, it will show that Jesus did not teach about a universal God. When he talked about God, he meant the God Israel worshipped during his time. That God was Yahweh. And neither the Jews, nor Jesus, believed Yahweh was the same as the Egyptian sun god Ra, the Roman Jupiter, the Greek Zeus, or the Babylonian Baal. Nor, of course, the same as the Islam's Allah, for Islam did not yet exist in his time. Nor the Hindu's Brahman, although Hinduism pre-existed Judaism. The God Jesus originally worshipped was not universal, but local and ethnic.

Yahweh was the warrior-god of ancient Israel. And his paradise was not extraterrestrial but mundane. That paradise was the ancient Israel transformed into the global religious-political superpower, greater than the Roman Empire. The worship of Yahweh existed probably at least three hundred years before ancient Israel emerged. It could have been brought to the ancient Israel settlement by Moses, a Midianite, through his father-in-law, who was a Midianite priest of Yahweh.

In essence, the God Jesus worshipped, was not the same as the God Christians now worship! Christianity invented its own signature brand of God and Heaven that Jesus did not believe in. The Christian God is the Father-God of Jesus, plus the deified Jesus, plus the deified Holy Spirit—that is equal to one new universal God, accessible only through Christian teachings and ritual. Universal, yet only Christian? One, yet actually three? A really confusing God!

When Christians say God, they mean the God they created. Not the Moslem, Jewish, Hindu, Chinese, Japanese, Native American, or Aztec God. Why? Because, as in any other theistic religion, Christianity also intends to colonize the world with its own God. There's no place for other Gods, or other religions, in Jesus' Kingdom.

And the Christian paradise? Again a confusion—a duality of a place up in the sky where God lives, and the Earth made new at Jesus' soon return. Probably a utopia of floating space or a huge planet. Check out this paradise madness:

First, Jesus' soon return did not happen, since he first promised it, when his original disciples were still alive. So Christians kept on postponing the event, and continue even now, a couple of thousand years later. Many Christian oracles have enriched themselves exploiting believers' obsession of that soon return.

Second, why would an omniscient God take the hassle of totally destroying Earth before recreating it? When he could just voice-activate the re-creation, as he did at the creation? While the Catholic Heaven, is more direct; if you're good, you'll zoom to the celestial realm. The Protestants Heaven still need to wait for that apocalyptic time when the Earth will be made Hell then made Heaven.

Third, whose paradise is right? The Catholic's celestial realm, or the Protestant's totally renovated Earth? If it's the Protestant, then evangelicals should start renovating the Earth now and let God finish it later. If it's the Catholic, then the Catholics should rather congratulate the bereaved for early retirement to paradise rather than condole them for losing life on Earth.

The fact remains, though, that the writer of Revelation was writing an imaginative cathartic fiction—expressing the then common believers' wish for a utopia beyond their inhuman persecution.

Back to Jesus. Jesus was merely focused on propagating social-moral values, especially the uplifting of the common people who had been downgraded to the fringes by state religion. Despite worshipping Yahweh, he was not into warfare. He was a social-moral reformer, rather than a political warlord. He redirected spirituality into something practical, rather than philosophical and mystical. And his cause was local. Although, as in any moral cause, we can deduce universal reapplication. While worshipping Yahweh, he did not also wage war against the gods and goddess of the Romans, the Greeks, or Egyptians. He was more religiously peaceful than his Christian followers who perpetrated inhuman religious colonization.

Interestingly, his paradise was the ancient Jewish society, morally and socially renewed. Not the exclusive extraterrestrial or terrestrial utopia reserved only for Christian church members. He was passionate about the social-moral reformation of the ancient

Israel. A socially and morally renewed ancient Israel was the new kingdom of Yahweh he envisioned to rise. Jesus was transforming Yahweh from a warrior-god to the God of social transformation.

Jesus' followers after his death, the destruction of Jerusalem, and their persecution, were groping for comfort and hope amid the uncertainty of life and looming death. Then, amidst their struggles, they discovered ideas that could be balms for their troubled souls: the ideas of resurrection, deification, and extraterrestrial paradise. These ideas were already present in other religions (Babylonian, Egyptian, Romans, and Greeks) during, and before, their time. So the belief that Jesus did not actually remain dead, but was resurrected and deified as God—emerged to give them hope in the afterlife, should they lose their lives in the present. They also adopted the belief of Jesus preparing a new paradise beyond this hopeless turbulent world.

The notion of Jesus' resurrection (a god, less mythical than a Greek or Roman deity), and the idea of Christian paradise, gained popularity among the Jews, Romans, and other people, because it nurtured hope beyond death. It was a belief so crucial amid a very tumultuous world, where lives were cheapened by the whims and wishes of emperors and warlords. With its growing patronage, the concept of Jesus' original Jewish social paradise, evolved into a universal extraterrestrial utopia. And a paradise open to all peoples of the Roman Empire. But accessible only to those who would become part of the then evolving belief system.

So, how could one become part of the belief system? Early Christians saw the need for religious initiation and membership rites, common in their times. They adapted the rituals already practiced by other religions, like indoctrination, or the initiation of the catechumens, and baptism. Gnostic religions were known for their knowledge rites and indoctrination, from whom Christians imitated. Note also that Jesus' baptism was not Christian. There was no Christianity yet in his time. His baptism by John was an ascetic Jewish religious practice. Baptism was also common in Roman cults. Contrary to the popular Christian notion that Christianity originated baptism; Christianity, instead, adopted baptism from other religions. And to keep the converts in their new fellowship, they modified the Lord's Supper into a religious fellowship ritual. Originally, the Lord's Supper was a humanitarian meal, where the haves shared food for the have-nots.

After affirming Christian beliefs and participating in rituals, converts were assured of paradise awaiting them in case of death. But, as they toiled through life, they were also assured that the deified Jesus was watching over them every minute of their lives. Inexplicable, though. What's the need for a God who watches his believers suffer and does nothing different had they not worshipped him?

So paradise is easily attainable by simply affirming the truthfulness of Christian beliefs and participating in church rituals? Seemingly easy. But then came the obsession for more details of God, Jesus, and Heaven. To be certain of God and Heaven, the pioneering self-made Christian theologians thought it should be detailed. Further constructions and reconstructions of a seemingly simple religious system mushroomed. Oftentimes, resulting in inhumanity among competing theorists. Succeeding generations of Christians become stubborn and brutally sectarian. Religiously insane of God and Heaven.

After contemplating on the nature of Christian beliefs about God and Heaven, I realized these notions have not really existed since the beginning of time. These were not handed down by a supernatural being called God to Christians. Christian faith is the product of theoretical constructions and reconstructions. And, like any other religion, Christian Faith had mundane origin. What the churches of Christianity claim as God is nothing but a theoretical characterization of what they imagined God to be. The Heaven they promise is nothing but a portrayal of what they fantasized utopia to be.

However, I also realized that these beliefs have become deeply embedded in believers' psyches—hardened by years of constant indoctrination. And disavowing it requires not just the courage to overcome group stigmatization, but also the courage to overcome the fear of the looming curse expected to befall disavowing believers! Freedom from such ideological enslavement is not easy. And, ironically, believers, instead of wishing to be free, end up strengthening their convictions.

In their endeavors to strengthen their belief system, theological pioneers emerged. These pioneers, starting from the Church Fathers, formulated and reformulated Christian beliefs into a more complex religious ideology. Proponents naturally integrated their varied cultural and personal backgrounds, including their respective personal preconceived notions. This resulted in the emergence of varied and, oftentimes, conflicting views. Christianity become confounded and complex. More so, when the Christian movement became an organized church. When competing theological proponents gained their respective followers, separate churches emerged.

And to make believers even more certain of God and Heaven, the churches of Christianity vied for exclusive rights to Jesus and the paradise he offered. This competition gave rise to further ecclesial entrepreneurship, resulting in an endless emergence of competing ecclesial franchises. Each offering what it regarded as the distinct and exclusive right to ensure humanity's fragile future. Fragile, because of the end-of-the world mentality.

So, the emergence of competing brands of Christianity inflicted further complications in believers' psyches. Believers ended up having the following religious syndromes:

One.

A delusion that one's hereafter is assured, and God takes care of his believers every day of their lives. Despite the fact, that there's no actual difference between the fate of Christians and non-Christians, religious and secular alike. Tragedies and bliss come to us regardless of religion.

Two.

Psychological enslavement to a belief system that perpetuates exploitation of believers' consciences and money. Believers are conditioned to think that a curse will befall them if they stop attending church services or stop giving money to their glamorous church and clergy.

Three.

Social-psychological exclusivism resulting from believers' conviction that their belief system is the only means mandated by God to connect with Him and be assured of Heaven. As Augustine said, "Outside the Church there is no salvation." By that he meant the Catholic Church, of course.

Four.

Cultural imperialism, because of believers' passion of changing the world according to their religious-cultural notions, from dress codes to sex, and even politics and racial biases.

Five.

Social interventionism, resulting from believers' conviction that they are divinely mandated to propagate their distinct notions of God and paradise, and turn this world into their church's kingdom.

While the world created products to make life more convenient, to trade and sell food, goods, and services necessary for daily life, the church was able to successfully market the notion of a supernatural being and a utopia beyond death, and exploit a big chunk of the human race.

There is nothing more culturally breathtaking than seeing our modern society finally freed from the long years of enslavement by the church in particular, and religion in general.

2
Franchising the Hereafter

Can everyone be assured of the hereafter? The church says so. But how? And which church?

The how, of course, is the theological product of the churches of Christianity. The how varies from church to church, and is the institutional core of each church brand. And the world is flooded with the incessant emergence of diverse arrays of church brands, combined with a dizzying number of sub-brands. Christianity is loaded, and randomly reloaded, with religious entrepreneurs offering what they claim as the best and most exclusive rights to the paradise of the hereafter.

Let's take a common sense look at the samples of these brands and their respective how-to-get-to-paradise theological products.

First.

Within the Catholic Church, the Patheos library lists 547 formed Catholic orders. They range from the famous Jesuits and Dominicans, to the lesser known Minims and Baladites—each of them having varied approaches to spirituality in ensuring one's paradisaic destiny beyond the present life. Some propagate monasticism, while others social activism.

But, generally, Catholics believe that the basic requirement to Heaven is infant baptism. Then, as adults, regularly partaking of the Communion that literally transforms itself into the body and blood of Jesus while imparting God's grace. That's gruesome, though! Confession of sin is another way to get rid of one's dirty soul that, otherwise, God's grace cannot override. Penance also complements divine grace, depicting a God who loves to see his believers both joyful and suffering—a split personality consistent with clergymen who preach about the self-sacrificing Jesus, but live in opulence.

The Catholic Church franchise in based on the notion that it can trace its origin to Peter, who Catholics believe was entrusted by Jesus to build the Christian church. As the church at the center of the then global power, and institutionalized as the official religion of Rome in 313 CE, it eventually eclipsed other churches, including those in Greece, Africa, and other Middle East. It further solidified its political dominance in Christianity when the Papal Rome achieved its "divine" foothold among the kingdoms of the world.

As the Roman Catholic Church became the leading brand of Christianity, its slogan became, "Outside the Church, there is no salvation." It claims that, as the only true church on Earth, only it has the authority to open both the gates of Hell and the gates of Heaven. Notwithstanding the fact that all the churches boldly claim unique rights to Heaven and to send others to Hell.

The Catholic franchise offers the wafer and the wine as the main product for the weekly maintenance of one's reservation of a piece of land and life insurance in the afterlife. This wafer and wine alone have yielded billions of dollars, or Euros, in terms of money, real estate, art, antique collections, stocks, and many more worldly materials collected since 313 CE. And the wealth keeps coming since then, even amid this world of hunger and poverty. In Germany alone, in 2013 alone, the Catholic Church collected a whopping $7.18 billion in state-imposed funding.[1] What a holy coffer!

Second.

An offshoot from the Catholic Church, the Protestant churches. Not one, but a huge number of them. Its three major slogans are, "The Bible and the Bible alone," "By grace alone," and "By faith alone." These diverse exclusivist "alone" slogans, resulted not only in the decentralization of one Protestant church, but also in the emergence of varied and competing Protestants churches. And every one claiming not only to be more truthful than the Catholic, but also more truthful than other Protestants.

But all agreed that the only basic medium for ensuring one's place in paradise, was the profession of Jesus as personal savior sealed by adult baptism. And what's the paradise? Well, Protestants made it simpler by doing away with the Catholic purgatory, an enigmatic holding place between Heaven and Hell. So one either goes to Heaven or Hell. No more purgatory that proved very financially profitable for Catholics in the Medieval Ages through the sale of indulgences—a piece of crap paper for upgrading dead loved ones from purgatory to Heaven.

The Protestant's franchise is based on the notion that salvation is a gift. And humans just need to sincerely accept it through the rite of adult baptism. But before accepting Jesus, one should first be converted from a sinful human to a righteous one. Acceptance of Jesus and conversion can also go together. Whatever that conversion means is really full of nuances and enigma.

So what are the distinct religious services and products Protestants offer? Well, teaching the Bible, not previously offered by Catholics. And making the Bible, that was previously a taboo in Catholicism, a public literature. Because human thinking varies individually, so Protestants also ended up having varied oracles of God. Each of them propagated their own signature theoretical products. Those notions of faith then became the foundations upon which their respective followers established their diverse and competing church corporations.

Financial exploitation in Protestant churches is more dogged than in the Catholic. While in Catholic church, tithes, or giving 10% of one's income, and offerings are voluntary. In most Protestant churches, these are required.

The emergence of Protestantism as a revolt against the Catholic Church, and as a movement of freewheeling unregulated church entrepreneurship—resulted in very inhuman religious wars between the Catholics and the Protestants, and among the Protestants themselves. The Christian's quest for franchising Heaven and God, ended up plaguing Earth with religious cruelties. The pages of our civilization's history are littered with the blood of believers who killed one another in the name of a God, they ironically portrayed as loving. The cause they envisioned as sacred and paradisiacal, drove them to make a Hell out of Earth. This simply reveals that church movements aren't divine at all. On the contrary, they are very worldly, and, at times, inhuman.

Third.

The Pentecostals, an offshoot of Protestantism. The Pentecostals are contemporary Protestants with trances and stunts. Their unique hallmark is "speaking in tongues" or a mumbling of words with, or without, trance. Rap could have been cooler! They also practice slaying of the Spirit, a less brutal form of slaying, but still posing a threat of head concussions upon falling on the floor.

Their service offerings include healing, and sometimes exorcism. I'm puzzled, though. Why don't miracle healers visit hospitals and just scream healing to all the sick from one hospital to another. That could save the world a lot of money and misery. What a heck of miracle will that be! Is it because people in the hospital who call themselves sick are really sick, so the trick won't work? And why not exorcise the demons out of all cruel dictators and warlords in the world? That would save our civilization a lot of precious human lives. That will be another heck of miracle!

The Pentecostal paradise is still the same as the Prot-estant one, although Pentecostals are still pettily squabbling among themselves as to when the paradise will come—before, during, or after the rests of the world will turn into Hell? And how to get to Heaven the Pentecostal way? First, accept Jesus as God. Then to be surer of Heaven "speak in tongues" or mumble your way to Heaven. A holy rap could be more poetic.

Fourth.

All sorts of what theologians call sects, that are actually, no different than churches or denominations, for all churches are sectarian anyway. They are the likes of Jehovah's Witness, Mormons, and Seventh-Day Adventist, among many others.

The Center for the Global Christianity estimated there were about 34,000 denominations in 2000, and about 43,000 in 2012. Really, it's insane to expound the notions of each of these ridiculous Christian churches, with each claiming to offer the most reliable means of ensuring one's place in paradise. The sheer number alone tells how ludicrous franchising God and the paradise is. Even Jesus would be stricken with lunacy just considering which among the squabbling churches to choose from. The probability of astronomers finding a planet that's ideal for human life is saner than the paradise in the hereafter being offered by these more than 43,000 religious entrepreneurs.

By why do believers buy it?

One.

Because they are conditioned to believe so, and have traded their use of common sense with cognitive blindness and irrational fear.

Two.

They feel that if they come out of their

sectarian confinements, they won't have a circle of friends to support them as they face the challenges of life, while also presuming the world outside is hostile.

Three.

They believe their sectarian notions are handed to them directly by God. They just can't realize that their beliefs are products of cultural carryovers and human theoretical formulations. There's nothing supernatural in religion, nor with what Christianity offers.

Four.

As moviegoers are hooked to special effects, despite knowing it's all a matter of green screen, believers find comfort in a fantasy of paradise in the afterlife amid the present turmoil and uncertainty of life. Like Hollywood, the church's business of offering fantasy thrives on catharsis for believers.

However, unlike Hollywood, franchising Heaven is an even more lucrative business, with only the notions of God and the paradise as core products—and that's easier to produce. And more delusional than the illusions of Hollywood, with church imposing its myths upon its adherents as real.

Five.

Because the church, like other religious institutions, for thousands of years, has successfully marketed the fear of losing one's soul and the claim for the sole solution to the fear. It has succeeded in making people believe that only the God it created can save them from doom. If people don't revere their God, they will be doomed to Hell everlasting.

Ironically, many modern societies still revere religion, and even endow it with special privileges, like tax breaks and laws against criticism, further institutionalizing the fear of rejecting religious myths.

Churches have enriched themselves exploiting people's fear of losing their souls, and offering the delusion of exclusive rights to Heaven. But a large chunk of our human race has failed to realize the stupidity of committing their lives to the myths of God and the fantasy of the hereafter. Essentially, there's no difference between what our modern society calls ancient myths of gods and goddesses, and modern-day religions, like Christianity. They are all products of imaginative ancient literatures.

The business of offering modern humans the ancient fantasy of the hereafter, is one of the most ridiculous ironies our civilized society still passionately patronizes.

3
The Notion of Sin and the Manipulation of Conscience

Is there really a God incessantly monitoring our sins? Monitoring more than seven billion of us, aside from our descendants, from the *homo erectus* to the Neanderthals, then to the *homo sapiens sapiens* long before Jesus came? And recording the details of our sins, past and present? What a deep intrusion into our privacy, making NSA snooping very trivial. And how does he do it? By the book? Actually, in the biblical cultural context, by the scroll. Man, what a heck of a lot of writing that would be!

And what's really the sin that he keeps on monitoring from us?

I'll eschew the petty theological expositions of sin. Instead, let's take an overview of the generic sin churches impose, the Ten Commandments, upon which diverse sectarian sub-sins are created.

So here's the Ten Commandments:

One.

Monotheism, or having no other gods than the God of ancient Israel, which was Yahweh. Here, Christians already violate the

First Commandment by worshipping Jesus as God, instead of Yahweh.

Two.

No sculptured relics. No wonder the Protestants condemned the Catholics for developing the art of religious sculpting. Protestants, though, substituted sculpture with painting. I guess Protestants just developed more love to the paintings of Raphael more than sculptures of Donatello. Although, Leonardo da Vince and Michelangelo, who were painters and sculptors at the same time, might end up puzzled, if not depressed, thinking of what makes one more wicked than the other.

Three.

Reverence of God. I think God has a problem with calling names. But wait a minute, let's take this scenario: what about impersonating God? Imagine portraying the Pope as the butcher Idi Amin or vice versa. That's ridiculous. But that's comparing a good apple with a rotten tomato. What about comparing a good apple with good apple? Say, portraying Obama as the Pope and vice versa? Imagine Obama having a shaved head and wearing a zucchetto and blessing the Congress with the sign of the cross. And the Pope having a groovy haircut and wearing an American suit, meeting the cardinals on a golf course. That's silly.

What about portraying the Old Testament's non-human Yahweh as the human Jesus and vice versa? For Moses and the believers of the Torah, that's not only ridiculous and silly, that's, above all, a blasphemy.

Four.

Weekly Sabbath breaks. This commandment also includes condoning slavery. But above all it means, that you guys and gals not taking breaks on Saturdays are sinful, and will be ferried by angels to Hell. Although Hell, being more tropical, can be livelier than the boring Heaven. Unless you're in the core of the lake of fire.

Five.

Honoring parents. I totally agree. So do Christians and non-Christian alike.

Six.

Abhorrence of killing. Whoa! Christians willfully did that to one another. Thousands of barrels of blood were spilled by Christians in the name of God, following the example of believers of Yahweh in the Old Testament times, not minding whether it was the blood of defeated soldiers, helpless women, or innocent children. Horrible! Yet holy?

Seven.

No adulterous affairs. But polygamy is okay. Only polygyny though. It's okay for a man to have more than one wife. Not polyandry, or a woman having more than one husband. That's unfair and gender discriminating. Men can have variations, while women suffer monotony? What about a church full of pedophiles? Still a holy church? I don't get it!

Eight.

No stealing. Okay, great! But what about enslaving the poor and hungry to build magnificent cathedrals that, ironically, awe many even today? What about relentlessly exploiting those who barely make ends meet, so their pastors can live in mansions and flaunt their glittering jewelries and high fashion suits?

Nine.

No false accusations. Cool! What about deeming one another as false churches? Each church making people believe it's the only true church, and others false.

Ten.

No covetousness. See how rich most churches are? See the pomp? That's the heavenly coveting the worldly! And not just coveting material goods, but also worldly political influence and power. Since Papal Rome started the trend, churches have always been covetously lurking to maneuver earthly governments.

So, after all the extravaganza of holiness, the churches of Christianity, by virtue of its moral canon, are as sinful as the sinful seculars. Does God monitor the sins of the churches also? Or is the Big Brother-God created by the church as a tool to manipulate the consciences of its members?

Back to the idea of sins. Let's take a glimpse of the branded sectarian sins churches have created.

One.

The Catholic. The Catholic has lots of sins. But let's pick a sample for practical purpose: the use of contraception. It's sinful for Catholics to prevent the birth of kids who will suffer in poverty and hunger. It's more righteous for them to see kids living in deprivation. And how could Jesus call the use of condoms and IUD's wicked, when there were no IUD's or condoms during his time.

Another one: the sinfulness of priests getting married. And as collateral, the righteousness of suppressing holy men's sexual urges. No wonder a number became pedophiles.

If marriage is evil, God could have not sacredly instituted it in the pre-sinful Garden of Eden. If sex is evil, then God should have created Adam and Eve with no sexual organs. Sexual organs didn't just pop from Adam and Eve with the invention of sin. Well, if we follow the notion that sexless life is holy, probably our world population would be contained. If not disappearing! Or, our world will be filled with neurotic couples walking like zombies. Staring at one another, trying hard to suppress their imploding sexual urges. Wanting to be intimate, but with grave reluctance. And ending up just gesturing with their hands while sighing, "I'm holy, after all!"

Two.

Okay, let's tweet about Protestant sins. There's a lot of them as well. But let's pick the Protestant's anti-Catholic sin-brand, like no sculptures in the church, only paintings. No praying to saints, only to Jesus. No sex outside marriage, just keep it private, only psychotics do it in public anyway. No killing, but Protestants can sing "Onward Christian Soldiers," before killing Catholics and other Protestants too. No lying, but it's okay to tell people they'll be robbing God should church members falter in paying tithes.

Three.

Let's chat about some of Christianity's weirdest sectarian branded sins.

It's sinful to Jehovah's Witnesses to eat blood. Okay, that's yucky anyway. Although, some cultures have food cooked in blood soup. But blood transfusion is not the same as eating blood. And it's more righteous to let a loved one die from lack of blood than to save him or her by using a blood transfusion? That's more than euthanasia—that's killing. And where in the heck did God say that using blood transfusion to save lives is sinful? So for Jehovah's Witnesses, everybody whose lives have been saved by blood transfusions will end up in Hell. That's plain lunacy. And that's why medical interventions should be mandated as transcending religious beliefs.

For the Seventh-day Adventists (SDA), not attending church services on Saturday is a violation of the fourth Commandment. It means that everybody who goes to church on Sundays, although still worshipping Jesus, are sinful. And no work, no play, no leisure all day Saturday, from sunset Friday to sunset Saturday. Gosh! People living in northern Canada, Greenland, Iceland, Finland, Norway, Russia, and Sweden, among others, must have a quandary with God about sunset time keeping. By the way, eating pork is also a sin. So, for the Adventists, the good pro-poor Pope who eats pork chops is as sinful as the devil. So are most Americans who love bacon.

The Amish believe that fashion is devilish, so they patronize only one boring style. Technology is also evil. So they may hire a taxi driver to drive a taxi, a product of evil, but not drive it—to make themselves holy, while making the taxi driver sinful.

The list of branded sectarian sins is a litany of things "Weird or What?" as William Shatner might say. But what's the point here?

One.

The notions of sin propagated by the churches of Christianity are mostly trivial cultural prejudices. Our common sense does a much better job in distinguishing what's right and wrong.

Two.

Churches are propagating their respective branded sectarian sin to manipulate their members' thinking, to ensure their respective organizational survival and expansion.

Three.

Churches thrive by making people believe they are born sinful, so direly needing God. And by making people believe they are more righteous than others, by virtue of not violating their respective branded sins, they calculate to thrive more than their competitors in the market of human soul.

Four.

Once people become trapped patrons, the church further manipulates their members' consciences, even toward inhuman ends. Brainwashing church members to believe that awakening to their common sense, is the devil's insinuation and a rebellion against God. We find this not only in the cults, such as Jim Jones' People's Temple in Guyana and David Koresh's Branch Davidians, among others; but also in mainline churches. Believing they were doing God's will, Catholic clergies and soldiers tortured others whose beliefs differed from them. One of the most destructive wars in European history, the Thirty Years' War of 1618–1648, started as a war between Protestants and Catholics. It was a war rooted in vying for the exclusive rights to God and Heaven. Each believed the other was evil, not only because they claimed the rights themselves, but also because each side had a different sin-brand. Believers ended up committing themselves to insane causes they believed to be divine.

Five.

The concepts of sin and Hell, and the promise of Heaven in the afterlife, are the most exploitative inventions religion has created to perpetuate its foothold in the conscience of humanity. Unless we have the courage to free ourselves from religious slavery, our society will ever be at risk of being dehumanized by petty religious ideology.

If the God worshipped by Christians is true, and the righteousness the church offers is genuine, these should have made Christians, and especially their clergies, free from doing evil. But, on the contrary, we even find more cases of pedophilia in the church than in any secular institution, like schools, government, etc.

Financial exploitation in the church is also more blatant and bolder than in the secular world. In politics or the business world, people invest money so they may gain something more in return. In the church, people are driven by their exploited consciences to give money in return for nothing but a delusion of a mythical paradise.

When will believers awaken to the fact that there's really nothing holy in the church, except for an illusion of mystical ambience their minds have been conditioned to think of? The concept of the sinfulness of humanity, and the righteousness of the church, are the tools the church uses to manipulate people's consciences.

There's nothing more dramatic in the advancement of our intellectual freedom, than seeing ourselves freed from the fetters of religious myths!

4
The Exploitation of Conscience

We need to awaken our sensibilities to the commercialization of conscience. When believers give up control of their consciences to the church, the church finds them easy to exploit. So that faithful church members struggling in poverty still end up faithfully giving a tenth of their income, plus offerings, to the church—while their pastors enjoy luxuries and their church buildings compete for glamour.

The *Economist* estimates that the Catholic Church's revenues in 2010 were about $170 billion. And out of this, $3.3 billion was spent in America alone, over the last fifteen years, paying for the molestation and rape crimes of its holy priests. The *Economist* further comments on the Church's unethical practices: "... the financial mismanagement and questionable business practices would have seen widespread resignations at the top of any other public institution."[2]

Kristopher Morrison in his article "Wealth of Roman Catholic Church Impossible to Calculate" in the *National Post* highlighted these figures, showing a sample of the wealth of the Catholic Church:

1. 716,290 square kilometers of global land holdings.
2. $22.4 million in an almost 1 metric ton of gold owned by the Holy See in 2008.
3. 10 Vatican's foreign investment accounts in the 1990s alone, ranging from banking, insurance, chemicals, steel and real estate.[3]

Economy Watch cites examples of the opulence of non-Catholic men of God:[4]

1. Joel Osteen of Lakewood Church lives in a 17,000 square foot, $10.5 million mansion. He has an estimated net worth of $40 million.
2. Ed Young of Fellowship Church lives in a 10,000 square foot estate valued at $1.5 million and flies in an $8.4 million private jet. He receives an

annual salary of $1 million plus $240,000 housing allowance.

3. Creflo Dollar owns a $1 million house in Georgia, a $2.5 million townhouse in New York, two Rolls Royces, and a private jet.

The *Daily Mail*, while reporting on the arrest of Benny Hinn's son (probably a WWE fan) for beating up a deaf and dumb man during Benny's evangelistic-healing crusade, estimated the holy healer's wealth at about $40 million[5] with an alleged annual salary of $1.3 million.[6]

Yonggi Cho, founder of the world's largest megachurch with an estimated 1 million church members, was accused by thirty of his elders in November 2013 of bilking $500 million from church money.[7]

We can go on and on, enumerating an exhaustive list of religious celebrities who enriched themselves exploiting and commercializing the consciences of their followers—but most of their followers will likely remain enslaved. Why? Because they get a weekly pep talk and entertainment show. And their delusion of a secured afterlife through a false sense of righteousness as a result of patronizing their church brand—deeply inhibits them from awakening to common sense. Their minds are so conditioned that they can't see, or they refuse to see, the exploitation done to them. In fact, many believers even value their relationship with the church over relationships with their families.

During my younger days I even traded my childhood dream of a lucrative career for a delusion of saving people's souls as a clergyman. I wasted my time, my life, and my parent's hard-earned money for a fantasy of Heaven. My conscience was exploited and manipulated by the church, wanting to perpetuate a very profitable global business empire selling myths.

But what really is conscience?

The church would like us to believe that conscience is a medium through which God speaks to us. But who speaks? A supernatural benevolent CEO of the universe? No, the church itself! A societal institution that some societies created to propagate ancient myths adopted, and adapted, from preceding cultures. The church is a mundane institution, operated not by supernatural extraterrestrial beings devoid of wrongdoings and immorality, but by humans like any of us, garbed in an illusory celestial ambience that church members are conditioned to believe.

So, is there really a supernatural independent self that exists aside from our mind that God uses to speak to us? If there is, why do people in varied cultures have diverse and conflicting senses of what's religiously right and wrong? Does this mean that indeed there are many gods, with varying views of what's right and wrong, speaking to different peoples? The church wouldn't agree. Neither do I.

Conscience is an outlook in life resulting from a process of mental conditioning. That mental conditioning is indoctrination. With varied doctrines, people have varied religious consciences. But believers are deluded into thinking that God speaks to them. In reality, it's a reaction to a mindset programmed via sectarian indoctrination. That's why people coming from diverse religions or Christian denominations have different conscience-responses. A faithful Moslem or Seventh-day Adventist would have a bothered conscience eating luscious pork baby-back ribs, while Catholics would salivate.

Furthermore, conscience is institutionally attached. Church members fear the thought of leaving their sectarian confinement because they are conditioned to believe that a curse will befall them if they leave. A Catholic attending a special occasion in a Baptist church is not bothered by not coming back, but a faithful member of that Baptist church is. Likewise, a fundamentalist Baptist who regards the Catholic Church as apostate will have a bothered conscience attending even a special family occasion in a

Catholic Church, more so taking the Communion. While a faithful Catholics will have bothered consciences if not attending weekly church services and taking Communion.

Church members simply don't realize the fallibility of conscience. With the preacher's theatrics, accompanied by emotional (as in contemporary churches) or mystical (as in traditional churches) music every week, they smoothly become committed patrons of the church. The church, in turn, finds it easy to make lucrative profits out of them.

The world over, I have seen believers struggling to make ends meet still committing their hard-earned money to the church before taking care of their family's needs. I remember hearing from a radio broadcast during the 2008 global crisis, that while many large corporations were cutting jobs due to profit losses, most churches were either able to maintain their finances, or even increase them. During an interview, a woman said that no matter what happened in the world, or to her family, she wanted to be sure there was enough money in God's church.

For believers, ensuring the propagation of church doctrines is more important than buying the necessities and comforts of life. Commitment is even more intense among churches with a sense of being persecuted by imaginary conspirators outside its enclave. As well as among churches with quasi-superhero celebrity pastors, like miracle healers, charismatic speakers, or self-claimed oracles of God.

The innate human desire to survive, the church's promise of eternal security through the practice of righteousness—that include financially supporting the church for a lifetime—and society's bestowal of special treatment of religion, perpetuate the system of exploiting and commercializing of people's consciences. But what do I mean by "commercializing people's consciences?"

Aside from the feeling of guilt inculcated among believers when they become unfaithful in giving tithes and offerings to the church, there are also a wide array of products and services available, some laughable, others mere imitation of the secular, that followers feel impelled to patronize to enhance their righteous status before God. Examples are prayer towels (a genie-less fabric that will make Aladdin jealous), crucifixes blessed by holy water (guaranteed to drive the devil away, but not pedophile priests), varied versions of the Bible (the result of a language barrier between God and ancient scribes), CD's (some silly, others gruesome with phrases like "Washed by the blood"), books (where a lot of mega-church pastors earn more mega-dollars), and even bingo and raffle tickets (a modest alternative for those fearful of winning mega-lotto).

Is spending money for the church really a necessity of life, or a luxury the church invented so it could enjoy Heaven on Earth—while church members are encouraged to endure suffering so they can go to Heaven? If God needs earthly currency, which church is his? All the churches? If all, then there's no true or false church. If only one, I bet every church would claim to be that one.

It's really mind-boggling that in my early

days, I couldn't realize that my conscience was conditioned. I was deceived to think that by believing in my church's notion of the hereafter, my destiny would be ensured, so I dedicated my life to the church. I was even willing to be poor just so the church could be rich.

How I wish my parents were still alive. I grew up in a poor family. I remember how my parents struggled to give me a bright future. They hoped that someday, when they got old, they wouldn't be homeless (they couldn't afford to live in a seniors' home), and would have a caring son to look after them (as they took care of me).

But when I look back, now I can understand the despair they had when I imposed on them (despite their being occasionally religious), my desire to leave my college dream that offered me, and them, more prospects for an economic uplift. I was fooled into choosing theology to serve God and his church, saving people for eternity. I was insensible to the toils of my aging parents, working even harder to pay for my more expensive seminary education. After finishing study, I left them, in their old age, poor, uncertain, lonely, and struggling for their daily necessities—just so I could serve my imaginary God and the church that squandered my humanity.

My parents both passed away without their beloved son spending precious moments beside them. I was so preoccupied with my fantasy of heaven that I forgot I had a life to cherish on Earth. I was blinded to think that the church was more important than my own family. I thought promoting a particular theory of God and heaven was more important than having a good livelihood and spending time with my beloved parents. I cannot bring back the time lost, but I'm writing this so others deluded by the church won't fall prey anymore. Or if have already fallen prey, will have the courage to be free from the shackles of the God delusion.

Believers need to take a closer, and candid introspection of why they should commit their lives and finances to the church instead of their own, and their family's, well-being and comfort. Life is more beautiful when we learn to savor the joys and realities of everyday life, free from the delusion of the afterlife.

5
Tithes, Offerings, and Financial Exploitation

There is nothing more financially deceitful in religion than the practice of tithing. Church members are indoctrinated to think that withholding ten percent of their income is robbing God. If God is indeed God, why does he need earthly currency to save humanity? It just doesn't make sense.

And which church is his depository? All? If so, does that make all churches divinely approved? So, there's no need for varied denominations to exist, only one or a few will suffice. But certainly, every one of the more than 43,000 denominations in Christianity would fight to death, claiming to be that one, or among the select few.

Although some modern churches have already abandoned the concept of tithing, there are still a number who impose it on their members. Members of these tithe-exploiting churches are compelled, both through the use of their conditioned consciences and institutional sanctions (like expulsion from the church, regarded as the gateway to Heaven), to give 10% of their income (other churches require 10% of the gross income, the lenient ones just 10% of the net) to the church.

But what really is the origin of tithing? Tithing, of course, didn't originate from Jesus mandating his believers that the Triune God regularly needs human currency to sustain and expand their extraterrestrial kingdom. Tithing was both a secular and religious practice in the ancient Near East long before Abram or the lesser known Melchizedek were born (if they were indeed real historical persons). Abram, obviously, was not Christian. Neither was Melchizedek. But nor were they Jewish. The historical context of the story of Abram giving tithes to Melchizedek was quite before the establishment of the kingdom of Israel. In fact, Abram was Chaldean, and was worshipping what Christians would call pagan gods. So Abram was pagan, as was Melchizedek.

Thus, tithing originated as a pagan practice. If we follow the Christian fundamentalist's thinking that tithing is an important aspect of living a holy life, then they are, ironically, imposing paganism. Tithing was adopted by ancient Israel settlements as a civil-religious taxation, and then was adopted by Christian churches to ensure they always had money in their coffers. This is counter to the belief that tithing is a God-given requirement directly mandated by God to the church.

Although a number churches today no longer require tithes, there are still many like the Mormons, the Seventh-Day Adventist, and most Pentecostal churches, who continue to exploit their church members' consciences and pockets. One of the countless examples was stated in the case filed by Tom Phillips, a former Mormon bishop in England, who accused his church and its global bureaucracy of bilking people of $257 million from 2007 to 2013 as a requirement for membership in good standing[8].

Another way churches receive financing is through weekly offerings, aside from donations (in cash or kind) that are even more substantial than weekly offerings. Yes, these are voluntary. Christians might say, "Don't be so naïve. Every institution needs financial support to exist and deliver its services." The issue, however, is not about people's discretion about financially supporting a societal institution. *First*, it is about the nature of giving. Even the so-called voluntary offerings and donations are always conscience-driven.

Church members give, otherwise their conditioned consciences are bothered. *Second*, the type of services offered. What the church basically offers is nothing but a propagation of religious ideology based on ancient myths. And *third*, the span of financial commitment required. The church requires a lifelong of weekly tithing and offerings, aside from donations.

If the church is solely engaged in humanitarian services, or socially and economically empowering programs to uplift the poor, supporting it would be a worthy cause. But the church is merely engaged in propagating a particular notion of life in the hereafter, deluding people about healing miracles (particularly among the Pentecostals), and assuring present bliss to all church members as long as they continue supporting the church.

That's a scam that governments condone by giving churches tax breaks and other financial favors, that could have been used to uplift the well-being of deprived citizens. You find this in the Germany, US, UK, Canada, and other countries with a strong Christian influence. For example, in Canada (which I thought, is more secular than other Western industrialized countries), I came across a December 2013 baffling expose[9] indicating that a significant portion of the $50 million in federal money intended to create jobs amid a struggling economy and job losses in Ontario went to church building renovations.

In London, Ontario, with the third highest jobless rate in Canada[10], $60,000 of poverty-relief money went to West Park Baptist Church for upgrading its roof, and $3,200 went to Colborne Street United Church to upgrade its barrier-free door, plus $2,600 for its main floor entrance. In other parts of Ontario, $125,000 went to Reno's Progress Church of God (for its community center used for advancing its institutional growth), $67,250 to Toronto's St. Andrew's United Church (for upgrading, exterior, and lighting), and $23,750 to Delta's United Church (for a furnace and water tank replacement).

Ridiculously, however, this instance of Canadian provincial funding of churches, is dwarfed by Germany's state-funded home renovation of the bishop of Limburg. An outrageous $20,000 bathtub (must have contain a lot of holy water), a $500,000 built-in closet (man, so how much more does the collection of signature holy garbs cost?), and a $1.1 million landscaped gardens (sacrilegiously making the Garden of Eden a joke), for a total of a whopping $40 million! Holy! What a bling!

What a shame for the churches and the government, trading the welfare of its people for the infrastructural upgrading of institutions focusing on commercializing myths!

Another issue with the practice of giving church offerings is the emotional trauma that goes with it. People who missed giving weekly offerings, more so tithes, because they're struggling to make ends meet (from feeding their family to paying their kids' college education, to even enjoying a little comfort in life)—suffer from bothered consciences. And the church likes it! In fact, it's always emphasized that God's work supersedes any mundane, or even family, concerns. Church members are regularly indoctrinated to give money to the utmost of what they have so God's work (that is, propagating a belief system) may progress.

But take a closer look at the lifestyles, the homes, the cars, the jewelries, the suits, the comfort and luxuries most preachers enjoy compared to most of their church members. Compare the glamour of many church buildings to the homes of the common people. Is it divine to preach about the self-sacrificing pro-poor Jesus and then practice an egotistic and pompous life? Isn't it plain bilking? Church members, though, who are determined to live a holy life, and whose minds are being blinded by dogged indoctrination, just can't realize they are being exploited by their so-called oracles of God. Oracles whose worldly ambitions supersede that of most common people.

Christians might say that not all churches are like that. But compare the economic status and comfort of life the church bureaucracy and their clergies enjoy with the majority of their church members. You'll see that those who regard themselves servants of the modest Jesus have more mundane comforts and luxuries than most of their church members.

I say that because I have been there. I was one of those who were once insensitive to the economic struggles of my church members, while making sure my church coffers would always be full. Looking back, I feel nauseated at how passionate I was in promoting Heaven. I, and my church bureaucracy, then, made sure we enjoyed the comforts of earthly life while financially exploiting believers who refused to see the truth behind our holy facade. The love of money is the root of all evil, holy men preach. But, ironically, the church loves money more than their members. Seemingly, though, you can't keep believers from loving the church as well.

But do we really need the church to ensure our Heavenly destiny? Or, at the outset, do we really need to be engrossed in the afterlife? Why don't we just enjoy the bliss of the present? Do we truly need the church to tell us how to find everyday happiness? If so, Rick Warren's (the famous pastor who authored *Purpose Driven Life*) son could have found solution and meaning in his life instead of committing suicide.

Fulfillment and finding meaning in life is not an exclusive domain of the church. It's open to all humans who cherish life and creatively shape it into something beneficial to them and to others. In fact, human life becomes more thrilling and constructive outside the repression of religion. The pages of the history of our civilization (from science, to medicine, to politics, to culture, and even to geographical explorations), candidly say so. Religion, since its inception, has suppressed human progress, and even brutalized those who pioneered thinking outside the box. Notwithstanding the cruelty the religious inflicted upon one another.

Those who dared think beyond the confinements of religious myths became the icons of the advancement of our civilization. The divinity of the human race lies in its freedom to think and constructively shape life toward a desirable end. It's this kind of divinity that deserves the beneficial use of our resources.

6
Holy Clergy and their Sacrilegious Affairs

"**The church is** holy!" believers always affirm. And the Catholic Church has long declared, "Not merely holy, but infallible!"

But are not politics (from politicking on who will assume the top church position, to scheming governments to become church puppets), racism (such as preferential treatment, racial segregation), sexual discrimination and immorality (such as fraud, pedophilia)—also present in the church? What really makes the church holy?

Let's talk about the issue of race in the church. It's nonsense that it took the omniscient God, or Jesus, 167 years to realize that a black pastor can also lead the Southern Baptists.[11] Or a whopping 1400 years for the Anglicans to elect the first black archbishop[12]. And why did it take hundreds of years for Southern Baptists and the Methodists in colonial America to realize that enslaved Africans were as equally dignified human beings as European Christians were?

See who's dominating Christian theology? While the high-tech corporate world, like Microsoft (who just chose an Indian-American CEO), value the talents of all people regardless of ethnicity (or sex), Christianity's theological academia and leadership are still racially selective, despite the myriads of highly educated and experienced Latin, Asian, and African potentials. Does this mean that the God Christians worship is racially biased on who to endow access to his wisdom and revelation?

We see not only racial prejudice in the church, but also ethnocentrism. Missionaries regard Western culture as the basis of judging what's acceptable to God or not. From music to church dress code, forms of ritual and art, deportment and church policies are always based on their upbringing. Non-missionary cultures are labeled 'pagan,' thus originating from the devil. It's also silly to think that medieval European attire is holier compared to other costumes.

Has there really been a God revealing what the church should and should not do since its inception to the present? Or is it just humans like us with vested interests in every decision made?

What about romancing with politics? Holy! Nothing is more romantic and subtle in politics than the politics in, and by, the church. While secular politics is about power and money, politics for the church is more than that. It's about power, money, control of conscience, and the domination of the present world and the hereafter.

In secular politics, people join parties for business interests. When the church joins politics, it does so to colonize society into a kingdom of its mythical god. In secular politics, party members donate money during election campaigns. In the church, believers give money every week for life. In secular politics, party members scrutinize their leaders on his, or her, ability to deliver material outcomes. In church politics, clergies manipulate believers' thinking to accept whatever outcome. These mentalities make the church, and clergy politics, even more exploitative than the secular.

A concrete example is church politics in the Philippines. The Philippines have been dominated by the Catholic Church since 1521, when Magellan first planted the Catholic cross. Despite the constitutional provision for separation of church and state, the Catholic Church boldly and regularly endorses political candidates during elections, as it did last 2013 national election.[13] Another church known for bloc voting (that lures candidates who could afford its luxury), is the *Iglesia Ni Cristo* or INC (Church of Christ)[14]. This church imposes upon its members the list of candidates that its bureaucracy endorses as God's mandate.

And, of course, the pages of European and American history are loaded with church usurpation of secular government, and the church imposing its political propensity as God's will upon society. Inside the churches of Christianity, politics is as evil as what the churches do to the secular world. From the canonization (the selection of which writings to include) of the Bible (where opposing church leaders with less, or no, political influence, were either suppressed or brutality murdered), to the cruel persecution of fellow Christians (with no, or less, clout with empires, from ancient to medieval) using government forces, to filthy politicking during the election of church leadership (regarded as God's mandate).

What about gender discrimination? It's baffling to think of why gender discrimination in the church is the only one of its kind condoned by governments, human rights activists, and society in general. Why are women not ordained, unable to be church leaders in many churches? Because God said so? Or, patriarchs, in their chauvinistic insecurity, just regarding women as less divine than men?

Further, there's still a huge crowd of Christians who would praise God foreseeing homosexuals and lesbians groaning in the eternal lake of fire, while praying for their pedophile clergies to enjoy life in Heaven. Imagine having immortal pedophiles in paradise. That will be horrible for kids!

So are clergies holier than the common people? The church more sacred than other societal institutions? If we let the cloud of conditioned mentality dissipate, we could candidly say no. The sanctity that believers ascribe to the church and its clergy is nothing but a superstitious attribution. It's this attribution that has deluded our society for thousands of years, and perpetuated the exploitation of our souls.

7
God's Will and the Despicable Agenda

How do we know it's God's will and not merely what a church's oracle has calculated to say? And what really is God's will?

Let's see some famous, or infamous, examples of God's will proclaimed by self-claimed oracles of God.

Pat Robertson declared that it was God's will, or actually vengeance, to send Hurricane Katrina that killed more than 1,800 Americans and caused unprecedented havoc. Why? Because of the sins of New Orleans. Later, he also proclaimed that the Haiti earthquake, that killed more than 100,0000 precious human lives, was also God's will. Why? Because Haitians made a pact with the devil[15]. At the outset, why did God not destroy the Devil instead?

If the Haitians were able to make a pact with the Devil, how come God did not know where the Devil was hiding? Or, another one of those mysterious conspiracies, that, in the end, made God a psy-war loser. Now people will think that the loving God of the 700 Club is a cruel avenger, after all.

Another one. In 1981, Oral Roberts opened the City of Faith Medical and Research Center. According to him, that was exactly what God gave him. It would bring a breakthrough in cancer research.[16] In 1987, Roberts revealed his conversation (not sure though, if via a direct link, Skype, or online chats) with God. He said God warned him that should he not be able to raise $8 million dollars[17] in three months to save the City of Faith, God would take him home. By the way, if he believed in Heaven, he should have opted for being taken home instead. Roberts' followers, not wanting him to have an early retirement to paradise, raised $9 million dollars. In 1989 the City of Faith closed. God, despite seeing the future, did not see failure coming. Trick or treat?

Joseph Smith, a Mormon church prophet, in the 1840s, revealed that it was God's will that Mormons engage in plural marriage. Sorry, ladies, it was only for men. In 1890, Wilford Woodruff, a Mormon church president, decreed that God changed his mind, he doesn't like polygamy anymore.[18] An omniscient God with a changeable mind?

Pope Gregory, as the vicar of Christ (not just Christ's press secretary on Earth, but above all, the embodiment of the incarnated the celestial God on Earth), founded the Inquisition in 1227. A few years after, in 1252 Pope Innocent IV[19] (the succeeding vicar), regarded the torture of heretics as a divine mandate. So, in a passionate obedience to a loving God's will, the holy church horribly tortured those with theological suppositions different from the Pope's. From solitary confinement in chains, to excruciatingly pulling extremities apart while mutilating the body, to slow burning at the stake—holy men of God inflicted inhumanity while praising God in their hearts.

Those were forms of torture that even the most lunatic of governments today would nauseatingly abhor. The culture of religiously-rooted torture lasted for about 700 years. The Spanish Inquisition alone resulted in approximately 150,000 deaths.[20] That's a lot of people writhing in pain before death. But, also take note, that these punishments are less cruel than the Hell good-hearted Christians envision for non-Christians. How horribly painful, seeing billions of non-Christians writhing in pain that can never be assuaged, in the lake of eternal fire. That must be a huge lake. God's will?

What about the Old Testament God? It was a warrior God that led Moses to wipe out a settlement and kill not just the king and defeated soldiers, but also every man, woman, and child (Deuteronomy 2: 31-36), and then plunder their goods. Genocide led by God through his warlords is a standard plot in Old Testament stories. So is the jubilant worship that followed each brutality.

God's will? Or simply a deification of cruel conquest common in the ancient world obsessed with greed, violence, and domination? Or, at the outset, was there God? Or simply a created deity used as a tribal totem to excite the vile desires to conquer others in a world of kill or be killed?

What about the New Testament God? Well, he also craves torturous vengeance. And the Bible is not even content with just preparing a lake of fire for non-Christians. It even adds sulfur as in other Bible versions. Men, women, children, seniors, babies, and toddlers, while being burned by fire forever, will further have the acid to corrode their bodies. And how many of those will suffer this Christian doom? As numberless as the sands of the sea (Revelation 20: 7-15). Why can't Congress legislate against such torture?

All these are God's will? What a despicable mindset and a despicable God. In reality, this so-called God's will is merely a notion (some scary, others funny) of people who claim to be "oracles of God," but who are nothing but hallucinating fraudsters, if not insane tricksters.

Spot any claim of God's will, past and present, and you'll surely find licentious motive behind the seemingly guileless divine proclamation. It could be a political agenda, financial exploitation, obsession for power (both mystical or material), or even zealous vengeance. God's will is plainly and simply nothing but a glamorized conceptual gizmo used to ingeniously propagate either a mystical obsession, or material fantasy.

The churches of Christianity would be better off if they stopped declaring God's will and, just like Pope Francis, affirmed, "Who am I to judge?" and then deeply engaged in what God (or rather Morgan Freeman) in Evan Almighty, called "ARK's," or "Acts of Random Kindness."

8
The Sense of Sacredness and the Ambience Of Fear

Is there really such thing as sacred? Or is it just a matter of mystical ambience or superstitious beliefs that we attribute to things and people because our minds are conditioned to think so? Could the things and people we think of as sacred actually not have innate supernatural qualities, or powers, that make them sacred?

For example, in the biblical legend of the Ark of the Covenant, when people acted sacrilegiously by touching the Ark, they fell dead. It's believed the Ark housed God's presence and power. If the story were true, then the soldiers sent by the mighty Roman Empire to wreak havoc to the holy Temple of Jerusalem, where the Ark was kept, should have all fallen dead. And why hide the Ark (as other theologians historians supposed), when having housed God's presence and power, it could just destroy the invading enemies?

Further, if God was personally present in the settlement of ancient Israel, under Moses' leadership, governance could have been very efficient and productive. If ancient

Egypt could be prosperous, why couldn't the omniscient God do the same with ancient Israel? With omniscience and omnipotence combined, God could have created the most desirable setting of life for his people so that instead of rebelling against him (an indication of discontent), they could have just enjoyed the best of life under his superbly beneficial leadership. It's more viable to think that the ancient Israelites wanted to live normal, peaceful lives, happily raising families and enjoying the fruits of their labor, than it is to suppose they wanted to rebel for the sake of rebelling.

Could it be that what the church wants us to believe as sacred, such as the divine ordination of the clergies, sacred rites and objects, sanctified buildings, the Holy Bible, and, God, are tools used as a means to manipulate our thinking and way of life?

Let's take, for instance, the claim of divine ordination and the issue of child abuse in the church. Even the UN could not but intervene because of the gravity of the problem. If ordination engenders divinity in clergymen, they should have been transformed into purely moral men. But we know that's not the case. In fact, the clergy has proven itself to be a breeding ground for pedophiles that has no equivalent in secular professions. So what's divine in the church's "sacred rite" of ordination? Nothing, really, except for the superstition church members attach to it.

What about the holy Communion? At the outset, the New Testament Lord's Supper was very different from what the church now does. The New Testament Lord's Supper was a humanitarian meal intended to feed the hungry. It was a fellowship intended for those who have more than enough to share food with the have-nots (1 Corinthians 11). But for centuries now the Lord's Supper has been used as a church ritual to dispense exclusive mystical institutional blessings to church members.

For the Catholics, the wafer and the wine literally transform into the body and blood of Christ. If it's true, that's really quite gruesome. For other Christians, the bread and wine are symbols of the body and blood of Christ offered (as horrible as the Aztecs) for humanity's salvation.

But salvation from what and from whom? From sins? Sins against whom? Against God? Why can't he just forgive humanity, or help us recreate our human nature, not in the hereafter, but now? And why do we need a sacred wafer and wine to remind us of cruel ancient capital punishment? To then end up imagining ourselves cannibalizing Jesus.

And what's really sacred in the blessed bread and wine? Does it transform human nature from sinful to righteous? Does it make one holier than others who don't participate? If it does, the clergy who bless it could have been freed from sinfulness, but clergymen are no different from other humans. Similarly, the bread and wine are essentially no different from bread and wine bought in a grocery store.

If Communion bread and wine has supernatural powers to transform human nature, it could have transformed celibates into sexually numb beings. But, despite the many weekly Communions they officiate, a number of them remain salivating maniacs? From the brutalities of the past and the sectarian animosity of the present, to sexual and financial exploitations among others, the holy bread and wine have never washed out the sins of the church.

What about the sanctified places, like the church itself? No other human institution has become the site of such unprecedented sexual abuse, discrimination, financial exploitation, inhuman ideological imposition, political subjugation, and manipulation of people's minds more than the church. I don't need to elaborate further on this fact. The pages of our civilization's history are littered with the wickedness of the church.

If there is a God in sacred places like the church and the Vatican, *first*, he could have transformed all clergymen into real holy men. *Second*, he could have saved innocent and helpless kids from falling prey to merciless pedophiles. Imagine the trauma those kids suffer the rest of their lives because of the revered child abusers in the so-called sanctified place of God. *Third*, as in the case of the Vatican (the holiest of all Catholic places) sins are even condoned. A UN report bluntly said, "The Vatican 'systematically' adopted policies that allowed priests to rape and molest tens of thousands of children over decades..."[21] Non-Catholic churches have skeletons in their closets too.

Also, why are churches, if they are indeed God's houses, not spared from natural disasters? Is it because natural disasters are acts of God? He must then be angry with those churches he destroyed. What about

Christian churches destroyed by fundamentalist Muslims? Was the Christian God on vacation, or less powerful than Allah?

Now, let's take a look at the Holy Bible. For non-Catholics, nothing is holier than the Bible, believed to be the word of God. Some Christians even attribute supernatural power to it, like the power to drive the devil away.

Others believe that every word in the Bible was literally dictated by God, making God bilingual, but biased for Hebrew and Greek languages. The problem of this belief is that the New Testament alone has thousands of variations. Bart D. Ehrman, James A. Gray Distinguished Professor of Religious Studies at the University of North Carolina at Chapel Hill, in his book *Misquoting Jesus* estimated about 200,000 to 400,000 variants in millions of pages of the New Testament manuscripts.[22] Although scholars have varied estimates, all of them agree, based on the manuscripts discovered and available for study, that variations are nearly countless. That's aside from errors of copying in a pre-photocopier age, and habitual inclusion of varied scribal comments and views. At times, the scribes reproducing the manuscripts would insert their own comments and ideas that would become part of the manuscript.

So, far beyond the supposition of many lay church members, the Bible was not translated from a single manuscript handed by God to humans. Translators, according to their preferences, simply choose which manuscript to use as a basis for translation. With hundreds of thousands of variations, not only are there numerous variations in words, but also in thoughts. Fundamentalist Christians theorize that the original manuscript for the Bible was literally dictated by God. But this theory would imply that since the original manuscript cannot be found, what they now have is really an unreliable Bible.

So whether one believes in the sacredness of each biblical word or thought, it really doesn't matter. The fact is, the Bible is just like any other collection of ancient writings. Its deification by Christians does not really impart supernatural power to it, except an illusion of its mystical attributes.

Many Protestants and Pentecostal lay members assume the Bible is their very own denominational heritage from God. Forgetting that before there was Protestantism and Pentecostalism, there was Catholicism, and the Bible was first a Catholic literary heritage. Christians need to note, also, that before there was a Catholic Biblical heritage, there was the ancient mass of Christian writings—numerous writings that were not meant as a single compilation, but circulated as individual texts.

Furthermore, what the original disciples of Christ called the scriptures were obviously not the books we now call the Bible. For it did not yet exist in their time. Instead, it was a set of ancient Jewish literatures. These literatures were not ancient actual reports of the creation of the universe (my goodness, who could have been there to write the report), but a literary heritage adopted from previous ancient cultures, in the context of the formation of an emerging nation (ancient Israeli settlement).

Contrary to popular assumption of the divine origin of the Bible (as if the Bible came fresh from God as one complete book), the ancient Roman Catholic and Orthodox church leaders decided, according to their discretions based on their respective theological views, which of the ancient writings would be included in their canons. Hundreds of years later, Protestants also contended which books from the previous Catholic and Orthodox canons to include, or exclude, from the Protestant canon. And the reformers themselves had different convictions about which to include, or exclude, from the Protestant Bible.

So, aside from the dizzying number of variations in manuscripts, there were also a perplexing number of variations of what constituted the Bible from different traditions[23], such as Western (Catholic and Protestant), Eastern Orthodox (Greek, Slavonic, Georgian), Oriental Orthodox (Armenian, Syriac, Coptic, Tewahedo), and Assyrian—aside from varying reformers' Bibles.

Candidly, the Bible is a product of ideological disputes and institutional struggles for dominance in Christianity. The obsession to dominate the ideas of what God should say resulted in vicious wars among Christians, and inhuman Christianization of the world.

Christian Faith, like other religions, is loaded with all sorts of sacred objects and rites. From holy water that, if indeed was endowed with divine power could have wiped out the Black Death and saved about 75-200 million deaths in church-dominated Europe. To crucifixes blessed by holy water. Even holier versions of the Bible. And laughable modern day magical items, like prayer cloths.

But for what purpose? Frankly, to exploit people's fear of the unknown, their fear of the mythical devil, the fear of death, and even curses from God (for patronizing other religious approaches). Believers are hooked to the church's sacred products and services, fearing that should they eschew these sacred things, doom will befall them.

Exploiting people's fear is one of the most powerful tools for perpetuating control of the human psyche. It takes courage to be sensible human beings, free from the shackles of religious manipulations.

Worldly Conquest

9
Faith and the Depraved Passion

What really is faith? Is there an essential difference between faith in God and ideological conviction? Is faith necessary in the advancement of our human race? To probe these questions, let's take a look at the nature and consequences of faith.

These are the elements that constitute faith: a notion of supernatural unseen realities, objects of devotion, a sense of conviction, oracles, sacred writings or traditions, sacred places, rituals, and of course, believers.

Supernatural notion.

Supernatural unseen realities are, obviously, a supposition of what could exist beyond the natural world that we see and experience. Is the notion factual? Of course, not! It could be a pure fantasy, or a combination of reflection and fantasy. The latter is more like religion. From the myth of the creation of the world to the fantasy of the future, are all imaginations. This also includes the history of the prophets and the messages they proclaimed, written not as actual autobiographies, but fictionalized accounts intended to propagate the writer's mystical notion. This is true of biblical accounts.

What happens next is even more confounding. When people become believers of myth, and see a growing number of fellow believers, they further mythologize and expound the myths they believe in. This results in a cycle of further mythologization and exposition. The outcome is the development of several layers of myths. Eventually, the myth becomes regarded by believers as real. That's how religious belief systems emerge. That's how faith is formed.

So, religion is really a luxury in our human culture. Basically, it promotes the creation and recreation of—and adherence to—mythologized notions. And being a luxury, it also propagates an outlook and way of life beyond our normal daily life that's oriented toward a mythical world and a mythical future. Those who claim ownership of faith (prophets, clergies, and institutional centers like churches and seminaries) perpetuate an addictive hallucination of paradise in the afterlife among its adherents.

Once hooked, adherents find it hard to get free. Why? Not only because of fear of stigmatization (by believers who regard backsliders as outcasts) and isolation (from a secular world that offers no extensive support system for ex-religious), but, above all, the fear of the curse of God. Adherents are always fearful that should they forsake their belief system, God will either curse them or withdraw his protection from them. Thus, they feel they become very vulnerable to tragedies in life.

Our modern civilized world needs to realize that followers of religion are really enslaved and exploited human beings. Such slavery is the most subtle form of slavery, because people with vulnerable psyches are psychologically manipulated and financially exploited. Oftentimes, it's not just individuals who are manipulated and exploited, but whole families, and even generations of families.

Objects of devotion.

Along with formulating a notion of the supernatural unseen world, the creation of objects of devotion further weld believers together. A common object of devotion is, of course, the adoption of God. In Christianity, it's Jesus who is further adapted into varied sectarian notions. So, ironically, although Christians profess to believe only in one Jesus, in actual practice and outlook, Christians adhere to a sectarian Jesus.

See if a Catholic priest would be allowed to conduct the Lord's Supper (commemorating the universal graciousness of Jesus) in a Baptist church, and vice versa. For the churches of Christianity, Jesus has always been an exclusive object of devotion, and this exclusivist propensity has resulted in numerous conflicting franchises of Jesus.

Further, devotion to Jesus has been historically used by the churches of Christianity to dehumanize humanity. Let me cite just three examples among the many.

One: religious genocide. The history of Europe attests to this. Because of sectarian devotion to Jesus, Christians (Catholics against Protestants, Protestants among themselves, and mainline Christians against minorities) zealously tried to exterminate one another.

Two: political subjugation. In the past, emperors and empires, fearful of God sending their souls to Hell, fell prey to the whims and wishes of the church. And the inhuman abuses of the church against secular kingdoms were many. Today, churches, believing that the sectarian Jesus they worship is the ruler of the universe, are still as zealous as they were in the past about colonizing the world (that includes governments) into a kingdom of Jesus. From politics, to medical ethics, to pop culture, Christians see their devotion to Jesus as the driving force for converting the world into their domain.

Three: promoting misleading and degrading social characterization. As in many churches (like the Catholic and the Anglican), women are still regarded as less divine than men. Thus, women cannot be ordained as clergy, more so lead the church bureaucracy. That is blatant workplace discrimination. Plus, LGBT's are always condemned and even regarded not just as less human, but as wicked humans. The church has degraded the equal sanctity of human beings more than any secular institution.

A sense of conviction.

Believers, doggedly indoctrinated weekly for years, find it very difficult to get free from the conviction that seemingly forever binds them with the church. As do societies with a long heritage of church influence. Why? Because they have developed a chronic sense of guilt-controlled patronage—a form of ideological conviction that perpetuates subjection for life to religious beliefs, totems, and rituals.

Thus, even while struggling to make ends meet, common lay members still find themselves committed to giving money to the church despite their clergies enjoying luxurious lifestyles. Faithful church members who can barely repair their homes will even give their money for church beautification, believing they should take care of God's house before their own.

Religion-rooted conviction is so influential that societies today still invoke it to stir emotionally heightened commitments in pursuing collective momentous causes. We saw this when America first declared war against 911 terrorism—and vice versa, when terrorists declared war against infidels—divinizing ferocious inhumanity.

Oracles.

The list of self-proclaimed oracles of God (individuals and organizations) is unbelievably long. As is the list of the glaring insanities they inflicted: the heartless purging of those who held views different from the Church Fathers, the atrocities of the Papal Inquisition, the horrors of the Jim Jones' People's Temple and David Koresh's Branch Davidians, to the petty judgementalism of preachers like Pat Robertson (on natural disasters) and John Hagee's (hatred of secular people), among others.

Idi Amin was a horrible dictator, no doubt about that. But imagine how even more horrible had he the convictions of either Jim Jones or David Koresh. Imagine if Pat Robertson or John Hagee were God. God the Pat would then devastate other countries who were not members of the 700 Club. And God the John would deport all secular Americans to Hell. Imagine also the same role for Joyce Meyers or Creflo Dollar, among other kindred of mega-church pastors. They would squander the global economy for petty luxuries.

Etc.

Out of our human desire to control the forces of nature and rule the universe, we came up with myths. Written or collected by enterprising pioneers, these myths evolved into belief systems. With belief systems came the recognition of ancient writings as sacred, oracles named, holy places chosen, rituals devised, believers gathered, traditions established, until the belief systems, usually with the backing of political powers, became rooted societal institutions.

The belief systems then found legitimacy governing people's lives. So the story goes, the myth became human, dwelt among us, and became our God. Ironically, humans then created God according to their own images. In the end, we all worshipped the God we crafted.

Think it Through.

Our sense of what's good and bad, right and wrong, moral or immoral, are universal values that developed as part of our natural adaptation. Our values are never the exclusive creation of religions. On the contrary, it was the deviation from the essentials of our being finite humans, that led people to create religions. In our fantasy to tap supernatural powers in order to cope with overwhelming challenges of life, we created myths. But we ended up worshipping these myths and relegated our rational nobility to myths, so that instead of becoming masters of myths we became slaves to myths and the myth-makers.

From the ancient practice of Babylonian infanticide, to the Aztec's human sacrifice and Jesus' sacrificial death, coupled with believers' martyrdom-complex, religion offers a more depraved approach to coping with human life. Our rational and creative endeavors in science, technology, medicine and other branches of human knowledge, guided by our deep sense of collective benefit, would do more enhancement to human life than religion.

10
Evangelism and Cultural Imperialism

As in any other religion, Christianity is passionate about making converts throughout the world. In fact, its missionary passion is matched only by Islam.

Christians call their missionary passion evangelism, or spreading the good news—the news that Jesus has become the savior of humanity and he is coming back soon ('twas soon since thousand years ago) to reward believers of Christian Faith with paradise. Because of this good news, Christians feel duty-bound to convert the world, both secular and religious non-Christians, to Christianity.

Ironically, Christians also aim to convert one another, believing their respective denominations the only ones sanctioned by Jesus, though none of them existed during Jesus' time.

But behind the seemingly virtuous pursuit lies a crooked calculated "goodness." And I say this as a former clergyman and theologian who was zealously evangelistic. Evangelism is born out of a notion that, because the rest of humanity have different beliefs, they are doomed to Hell. Christians assume that people outside their respective churches are hopeless, God-less, and ignorant of the only way to Heaven. So they need to be saved by converting to Christianity.

Salvation, in Christian beliefs, is the present assurance of deliverance from the forthcoming eternally agonizing Hell the loving God has prepared for all those who reject Christian religious ideology. Such a God would make Mao and Stalin more saintly than him. Eternally excruciating pain in the lake of fire as punishment for breaking the Ten Commandments? That's really outrageously ruthless.

Even our modern societies are trending toward rehabilitation rather than ruthless punishment. Capital punishment in countries like the United States strives to not prolong the agony of convicts. Why can't God, in his omniscience and eternal love, create an alternative planet for sinner's rehabilitation with a system so efficient that sinners could not help but willfully desire righteousness? If he created the universe in the first place, he can also do that. And, contrary to the Christian profession of love, Christians look forward, with enthusiasm, to the day when non-Christians will forever writhe in extreme pain in the lake of fire.

But what really is evangelism? Making all people live according to the Ten Commandments? Peoples of all cultures have their sense of right and wrong. That sense of morality is one of our common human qualities. As in other theistic religions, the only reason Christianity wants to convert people to its faith is religious imperialism. Christianity sees itself as the only global norm of all religions and cultures.

Just see the silliness of how conversion works in Christianity. For Catholics, once an infant is baptized, bingo, he or she becomes a citizen of Heaven. Does that baptism ensure righteous life, from infancy to adulthood? The Protestant version, though, is more dramatic, with preaching, singing, altar call, then eventually adult baptism. At times baptismal candidates shed tears, carried by the hallucination of new life in Christ. The Pentecostal style is even more dramatic, with more revelry, screaming (probably to wake up a slumbering God), an adaptation of voodoo trances, and even tricky healing miracles. But will those dramatic shows ensure saintliness throughout life? The list of preachers living a luxurious life while bilking their poor members is long. As is the list adulterous pastors.

The so-called conversion experience in Protestantism and Pentecostalism is nothing supernatural, but merely an experience of emotional highs. That emotional high is common where the collective consciousness is stirred. We see this in secular motivational workshops, deeply moving films, concerts, and Olympic events, where an exhilarating experience touch our lives.

So, in essence, evangelism is, really, not about the concrete and verifiable salvation of humanity. Claiming to have the secret for saving the whole of humanity, past, present, and future, is just too ludicrous. Evangelism is about propagating a religious ideology along with a prescribed lifestyle. It's a form of ideological and cultural imperialism. Its purpose is to make people commit, first to a general Christian thinking, then to particular, denominational ideas.

That initial ideological commitment is intended to further perpetuate a whole gamut of institutional commitments, like bureaucratic policies do's and don'ts in everyday life, financial obligations, regular church attendance, participation in rituals, and affirming the truthfulness of congregational doctrines and fantasies of the afterlife, among others. Eventually, adherents are also urged to become evangelists themselves to further spread their denominational religious ideologies and lifestyles. And denominational loyalty is a must, an allegiance that transcends even national patriotism.

Evangelism nowadays has become a multi-million dollar enterprise, at times even supported by politicians wishing for congregational votes. We need to realize, though, that the obsession to convert the world to one's religious beliefs is an attempt to control people's thinking and ways of life.

Fairy Tales

11
Doctrinal Integrity

Are church doctrines made in Heaven? Believers think so of their respective denominational doctrines. They assume their respective doctrines came from the mind of God, and thus is the only truth.

Ignoring the fact that their doctrines were formulated by their denominational organizers, who were neither angels nor God. At the outset, their denominational pioneers offered a set of religious concepts they adopted from others. Then, other pioneers deliberated on the concepts, until they finally chose which concepts they should regard as God-given. Whatever suited their preconceived notions, they chose. Their chosen concepts were then baptized as divine doctrines. Bingo! You have now the secret of Heaven.

Subsequent new generations of denominational thinkers emerge. They further modify their doctrines to suit their changing cultural milieu, and, aha! new secrets of Heaven are now available to eager devotees. With doctrines come other institutional matters like rituals, codes of deportment, and organizational policies—all regarded as mandated by God.

However, at times denominational doctrinal deliberations become so heated, causing altercations, that sub-groups separate and eventually form new denominations. So, together with other pioneering religious entrepreneurs, Christianity is loaded, and reloaded, with all sorts of denominations, each claiming to be the only God-approved church.

Let's take a peek at the samples of denominational doctrinal beliefs.

Catholicism

Fundamental Belief: that Jesus himself established the Roman Catholic Church through the apostle Peter, and that outside the Church there is no salvation, as Augustine said. Although other Catholics nowadays seem open to God becoming merciful to non-Catholics, they still insist that, to be sure of Heaven, non-Catholics need to join the Church.

However, considering the Gospel account of Matthew 16 on the building of the church was a factual historical account, neither Jesus nor Peter had an inkling of what the Roman Catholic Church was. The Church came much later, when they were both long gone. If a claim of organizational origin from Jesus, after Jesus was long dead, is the basis of the truthfulness and originality of a church, then all churches who claim the same origin are also true and original.

In fact, the earliest church in Rome was one of the many earliest churches of Christianity during the Apostles' time. And there was no particular Peter's brand of the Christian church in New Testament times. There were churches located in various places, and were named according to their locations, but they were not denominational churches. So we find in the New Testament the church in Jerusalem, the church in Corinth or the Corinthians, the church in Ephesus or Ephesians, among others, aside from the churches in Africa and other places not directly mentioned in the Bible.

Moreover, the early churches were not religious institutions, they were fellowships of people. Some gathered in homes, others in places like riverbanks. The original churches of Christianity were not state-registered religious organizations, nor were they formal institutional structures with complex policies, salaried clergies, bureaucracies, and magnificent buildings. These institutional matters came hundreds of years later. So, an original disciple of Jesus, and even Jesus himself, would be shocked to see what the church looks like today. Claiming the earliest Christian origin as the basis of selling an exclusive right to a universal God and Heaven is, really, a bamboozling of people's hearts.

Supporting Belief: The Catholic Church inculcates in the mind of their members that weekly partaking of the Communion (the bread and the wine) is essential in obtaining God's grace. The ritual hooks believers for life, not realizing that if indeed the wafer and the wine is the source of God's grace, it would never be that fleeting to last only for a week, since God's grace is eternal.

Imagine how one feels missing God's grace for a week, more so leaving the Church and having no access to it forever. Thus believers are spiritually traumatized at the mere thought of leaving the Church.

The Lutherans.

Fundamental belief: Justification by "grace alone," through "faith alone," by "Christ alone." This doctrine is a blunt challenge to the Catholic's belief that the Church is the repository of God's grace. But how the Lutheran's theory of the process of transforming human nature works remains an enigma, even after five hundred of years of theological scholarship. And did Martin Luther's doctrine of righteousness by faith, indeed, make people righteous, or more righteous than the Catholics?

Martin Luther's ideas of divine righteousness resulted in inhuman religious-political revolutions and wars, ironically even among Lutherans themselves as in the Schmalkaldic War of 1546 to 1547, aside from the wars waged against other Christians. So did religious doctrines really came from God? Or were they products of ideological-political conflicts, by people disgruntled with their church, who formulated concepts to counter their church belief system?

Support Belief: the Bible as God's words. While the Lutherans seemingly rejected Catholic traditions, they still ended up imbibing Catholic heritage, from the Bible to the Communion, with just some revisions.

You see, theological development is all about whimsical formulation and reformulation of mystical concepts that, ridiculously, followers assume as a matter of life and death. Imagine if the time and effort wasted in mystical matters were, instead, spent in developing wisdom on how to make our world a more equitable and dignified place to live. The world, now deeply influenced by religion, could have been more divine.

The Calvinist or Reformed Church.

Fundamental Belief: each human being is predestined by God either to enjoy the cozy paradise beyond this Earthly life or forever groan in the lake of fire. This is the silliest of the major Christian traditions, because it tells believers that God had already predestined their fate even before they were born. So whether they worship God or not, it doesn't matter anymore. Then why be religious? If all of Christianity were like Calvinism, then the more enthusiasm atheists would have for their convictions. Because while Calvinists may depict atheists as having no hope in life by having no God, atheists obviously have reason to characterize Calvinist Christians as the walking dead.

Imagine worshipping a God who already predestined you to be saved or lost. And you don't know whether or not he predestined you to be saved. If he predestined you to be saved, why the heck would you still waste time worshipping him, you're saved anyway. If he predestined you to be damned in Hell, the more you should run away from him like the plague. The more you should curse the church for bringing such a God to Earth. But, well, cursing is rude, even for a decent atheist, so just think of it as a ridiculous religious scam born out of a silly ideology that people in the past were willing to kill and die for.

Support Belief: Use of musical instruments is idolatrous. Therefore, no musical instruments in the church. Calvin's God must have hated music and loved a cappella. But years later, followers were getting bored of a cappella. They were itching to hear full and enlivening music. So they contended with Calvin and came up with a revision of God's will. Now God loves music, complete with the luxury of instruments.

The Baptists.

Fundamental Belief: Baptism should be by immersion, and only for adults, in contrast to the Catholic's infant baptism through sprinkling. They argue that Jesus was baptized as an adult, not as an infant, and not by sprinkling, but by immersion. To follow Christ, all those who accept him as their savior need to be baptized by immersion. Baptism symbolizes death to the old self, full burial rites, and resurrection to a new life. Baptists argue that in burial we just don't sprinkle earth, but bury the dead underneath the earth.

So what will happen to the rest of Christians, more than a billion precious human lives, aside from the billions more before the Baptist church was organized, who are not baptized the Baptist way? Lost in Hell? If immersion is indeed the right way for people to experience divine transformation, why did it take 150 years (1845 to 1995) for the Southern Baptists to realize that enslaving fellow human beings is sinful? Such a very slow transformation eh?

Support Belief: As common to Prot-estants, Bible study is urged as a necessity in Christian life. So Baptists study the Bible like crazy. Some believe that the Bible is the literal word of God, while others believe it's not the words themselves, but the thoughts that are inspired by God. All believe, though, that the Bible is the revelation of God's will.

Thus, all Baptists who want to know God's will need to study the Bible. The result is a dizzying number of conflicting Baptist denominations, all claiming their respective Biblical ideas have been the will of God. What a confusing God, with confused followers.

Etc.

The Pentecostals declare that, as God has said, aside from water baptism, true Christians still need to have the baptism of the Spirit. I guess even the Trinity was contending with each other's incomplete ritual prescription. And what's the baptism of the Spirit all about? Basically, it's about mumbling words while in trance. At times it even includes being knocked down to the floor by the Spirit. If you saw it, you would think it cool pageantry though.

Mormons claim to have the updated version of the word of God. This time, though, it's not stone tablets, but cooler gold plates. One of the hip features: it's okay to be polygamous. But sorry, gals, it's only for guys. However, Mormons later revoked what God previously said. So now, sorry, guys, no more religiously legitimate spousal variations.

The Seventh-day Adventists insist that worshipping God on Saturday is holy, and worshipping on Sunday is devilish. Looks like God loves Saturn more than the sun. Jehovah's Witnesses preach that Jesus was human and not God. Okay, that sounds better. But God also forbids blood transfusions. Jehovah must have either loathed the Red Cross or seeing blood that he would rather humans die than save them with blood.

A wide array of other churches even have founders who claim to have magical powers which would make many Las Vegas magicians (except probably Copperfield) look like a novice—with a miraculous knack for making money in healing crusades and elaborate stage shows.

Time and page constraints, forbid me to cite more than just a glimpse of the more than 43,000 denominational beliefs. My goodness, how can adherents still stand the madness of believing in religious myths, let alone choose which one to believe in?

Theology and doctrines, despite what theologians call scholarly endeavors, are nothing but silly assumptions of what were already myths. It makes me wonder why there are still theology departments among our secular modern-day centers of science and technology. If I were to define theology and doctrinal formulation, I would reverently call it the mythologization of myths.

12
The Bible and its Holiness

What makes the Bible sacred? Is it inspired by God? Or Christians merely claim it to be? What makes it unique from other sacred writings? And who wrote it anyway? These are some of the issues that are crucial in knowing if the Bible really makes sense.

At the outset, I'm wondering why all sacred writings are ancient? Is it because ancient writings seem more mysterious and mystical than modern literatures? I'm inclined to think so. As in any other religion, the sense of sacredness attributed to a set of ancient writings is relative. The Bible is not sacred to the Muslims. Nor is the Quran to Christians. Or the Book of Mormon to Protestants.

This obviously indicates that the attribution of sacredness to a particular set of ancient writings is sectarian instead of a sole act of one universal God. Otherwise, there would just be one set of universal sacred writings, mandated by God, probably with thunder and lightning for emphasis. Then periodically affirmed by God in loud and clear and grand multilingual celestial presentations.

Of course, each religion argues for the validity of the divine origin of their religious canon. This contention results in the dogged dispute, not only about authenticity, but also over dominion of the God portrayed in their respective writings. Moreover, the God each religion claims as the true and the only one is also culturally ethnocentric. So we have the Hebrew-speaking God of the Hebrew Pentateuch, the Arabic-speaking God of the Arabic Quran, the Sanskrit-speaking God of the Sanskrit Vedas, the Japanese-speaking God of the Japanese Kojiki, and the Hebrew-speaking God of the bilingual Hebrew-Greek Bible (a Canadian would say, bilingual eh?).

So what makes the Bible sacred? Of course, nothing to the non-Christians. And for Christians, all of it. If a supernatural word-power is innate in the Bible, regardless of format: ancient scroll, modern hardbound, softbound, eBook, or audio book—everyone reading or hearing it (regardless of religious affiliation, or being religious or secular) should immediately sense an overwhelming life-transforming power. But this supernatural divine phenomenon does not universally happen. It is the same with other sacred canons. This really shows that no divine power resides in the Bible, or in any so-called sacred writing. Its sacredness is merely dependent on believers' relative attribution. It's all about attitude instead of inherent quality.

For example, there's nothing divine or life-changing reading Chronicles 1 and 2 in the Bible, with boring long lists of ancestral records. But when fundamentalist Christians read it, they read it as if there's really something mysteriously divine in reading the lists of unknown ancient families. It's nothing but plain superstition.

And very ironic are the numerous occurrences of immorality, genocide, and discrimination that are commended in the Bible, and even praised as divine by Christians, though abhorred by normal civilized people. Examples are:

Genocide.

Imagine the chosen holy people of God killing not just the soldiers of settlement they conquered, but ferociously slaughtering innocent babies and defenseless women and civilians, along with the inhumane butchering of cattle, sheep, goats, camels, and donkeys (1 Samuel 15: 1-3). In another instance, after killing all the soldiers in the battlefield, the warriors of God went back to the defenseless town and wiped out the entire population of 12,000 and plundered the goods. Then, not yet satisfied with the brutality, burned the town to ashes (Joshua 8:24-28). Imagine mothers screaming and wailing while their babies were butchered by the people of God. Imagine the helpless kids writhing in pain while God's chosen people rejoiced, slaying them with swords and spears. Imagine the neighboring towns seeing not just empty tables and empty chairs, but an empty town in ashes. Horrible and senseless!

And these are just two of numerous occurrences. The Bible is loaded with God-driven genocides. But Christians reading these genocides would praise God for giving his "holy people" the ferocious conquest they were salivating for. That's more than a cuckoo's, if not a maniac's, mentality.

Child Abuse.

What about offering virgin daughters to be gang-raped by sexual maniacs just to save two mighty angels of God (Genesis 19:1-8)? Ludicrous and nonsense! In the Holy Bible, women (most likely Lot's daughters were teenagers) can just be given by their parents to the mob to be gang-raped. Is that morally justifiable, and an instance of a holy story? That's maddening and insane.

Of course, Christians may argue that that's what Lot did, and not what the angels of God wanted. But what about incest practiced by Noah and others? What about the infanticide of Isaac by Abraham, although not consummated? And the practice of fathers giving daughters in marriage, like a commodity? Suppressing their daughter's freedom of choice. Ironically, Christians teach that freedom of choice is inviolable and universal to all human beings.

Slavery.

What about the New Testament? It also condones slavery (1 Timothy 2:12), that modern civilization now realizes is not divine. If the Bible is indeed God's word, intended to transform humanity into something more divine, it should not condone slavery. More so because slavery in New Testament times was really cruel.

Gender Discrimination.

1 Corinthians 14:34-35 and Ephesians 5:22 exemplify the imposition of gender discrimination. If you follow biblical principles, there can never be women professors, politicians, or CEO's. Moreover, women are biblically

mandated to be subjugated by their husbands. And LGBT's nowadays should be thankful they don't live in biblical times; otherwise, they'd be gone on Earth (as in Leviticus 20:13, Jude 1:7). Present-day fundamentalist Christians passionately agree.

Sadistic Revenge

The Book of Revelation is loaded with passion for an extreme form of revenge—throwing all enemies into an eternal lake of fire so they may writhe forever in the agony of being burned eternally without the privilege of dying. That's really appalling a revenge, that even the ancient Romans would be appalled to do. No civilized society, more so a divine one, would impose such capital punishment.

The real issue.

Some theologians would argue that because of the historical context of the Bible it contains social norms that are different from our modern civilized world. The real issue, though, is not about the literary, historical-cultural context, but the moral underpinnings. If God transcends the universe, he also transcends a speck of historical human culture. And if the Bible is his revealed will, that divine will should transcend the immorality and inhumanity of the biblical writers' time. Unbounded universal norms and practices that enhance the sacredness and dignity of human life, regardless of fleeting historical-cultural setting, should have been uplifted by the Bible.

Contrary to popular religious beliefs, the Bible, like other sacred canons, is an ethnocentric literature. Its main focus is the propagation of its adopted myths, not the promotion of universal human qualities; although it may teach human qualities related to the promotion of its myth.

The core of the stories in every sacred text is the myth of one's ancient ethnic religious supremacy. The so-called sacred scriptures were written by fantasizing ethnocentric self-claimed oracles with delusions of cultural grandeur, with no peer review verification of their writings. Sacred canons were written in the backdraft of the opposing peoples and cultures of their time.

That's also true of the Bible. The seemingly holy norms and practices found in biblical narratives are merely folkways practiced in biblical times. Most of these were assimilated from other cultures. It's intended to glorify the acts and beliefs of particular groups of people—the ancient Jews of the Old Testament, and the early Christians of the New Testament. Whatever acts and beliefs they had that comforted them in their miseries and advanced their causes, they regarded as divine, regardless of the moral implications.

So we find a lot of moral inconsistencies in the Bible. While it says no killing within its society, it also urges genocide against others. While is says no to adultery, it also accepts polygamy, and extramarital sex with slaves (as with Abraham and Hagar). While it says no to stealing, it also mandates God's people to plunder the goods of other settlements. While it promotes the love and mercy of Jesus, it also envisions ferocious vengeance against others who believe in other religions and who don't believe in religion at all.

The brainwashing that religion inculcated to human civilization for thousands of years has turned even modern and civilized people into moral schizophrenics—claiming to be moral while esteeming their own immorality.

13
The Earthliness of the Bible

Bible texts have context. They were not written out of a blank slate. They were written by people who had particular concerns about the immediate circumstances of their lives. They wrote about their struggles, their dreams, and their beliefs, adopted or adapted from their surrounding cultures.

And take an important note: the Bible that we now have is just a fraction of the body of ancient Jewish and ancient Christian writings.

So the context of the Bible is not modern human life. Using ancient writing as the basis for directing our modern life is like using Josephus' writings to interpret American history, or as a basis of interpreting what American society should be. Moses (although, many scholars doubt his authorship of the Pentateuch), Paul, and other writers of the Bible, did not have a clue about modern day ethical issues like medical, biotechnological, or even social ethics. Modern society now abhors slavery, while Biblical writers supported it. We don't stone to death, or crucify, people for trivial acts (like claiming to be God, or having homosexual affairs). Nor do we regard it sensible that the president of America heard the voice of God to annihilate Iraq.

What we now call biblical doctrines, or God's revelations, were products of ancient worldviews that if written today would really be ridiculous. Imagine if Bush declared war on Iraq not because of the alleged WMD's, but because he heard God telling him in the middle of the night that he should destroy Saddam Hussein. And not only kill Saddam, but wipe out the entirety of Iraq, and all its men, women, children, including animals, and burn it to ashes. That could have made the war in Iraq even filthier, and more outrageous too. But that was what happening in Old Testament times.

Imagine worshipping Criss Angel because of his magic tricks, or Benny Hinn because of his healing tricks, as God? And America declaring the worship of Angel or Hinn as the official religion. Writers then interpret all actions and words of Angel or Hinn as divine, and write all sorts of suppositions and myths about them. That's hilarious. But that's what Christianity has done in its deification of the human Jesus as God.

Theological suppositions are recycled, revised, argued, developed, and redeveloped, then tagged as God-given doctrines. There is even a so-called scholarly discipline of making further suppositions out of ancient suppositions, and arguing with one another on whose suppositions are approved by the mythical God. Christians call it theology.

Furthermore, when a Christian says he believes in the Bible, which Bible does he mean? The Bible was not a finished product handed by God to humans through extraterrestrial angels, now printed by modern machines and also posted on space-age websites.

First.

The Old Testament is not Christian. It's just Jewish, written by Jews, for the Jews, talking about Jewish heritage that's sacred to the Jews. Judaism does not believe that God can be incarnated. Jews who still believe in Judaism don't believe in Jesus as God. So the Torah does not really teach about Jesus.

Second.

There is not one, but many Bibles. Many Protestants, as well as other non-Catholic Christians, assume that the most popular form of the Bible is the original God-approved Bible. By the way, with a book containing 66 sub-books, fundamentalist Christians should feel eerie, because adding one more 6 would make it 666—the feared number of the Devil. They are ignorant, if not ignoring, of the history of the compilation of the Bible. If Christians think that the original compilation is sacred, then every Christian should accept the Catholic Bible as the original and most ancient form of Biblical compilation.

The fact is, aside from the hundreds of thousands of manuscript variations of each book included in the popular Protestant Bible, there are also varied Bibles with different books included. The Catholic Bible and Orthodox Bible, more ancient than the Protestant, included seventy-two books, plus other additions to Daniel, Esther, and Psalms. Take note, the Protestant movement began in the 1500s, so the Catholic-Orthodox Bible is more original than the Protestant. The Russian Orthodox Bible has 2 Esdras. The Ethiopian Orthodox Bible has Jubilees, Enoch, and Meqabyan. The Syriac Peshitta Bible has Psalms 152–155 and 2 Baruch.

Even Martin Luther, the father of Protestantism, did not accept the Books of James, Hebrews, Jude, and Revelation as inspired by God. But how did the present popular form of the Protestant Bible become regarded as the true and original Bible? Well, it simply became a religious-cultural tradition carried over from the non-Catholic Christianities—who then branded it as the God-given Bible. Just a matter of earthly branding, an example of how an earthly ancient literature, or sets of literatures, was deified.

Third.

The prophecies of the Bible are no different than the prophecies of Nostradamus or daily horoscope. They can all be interpreted and reinterpreted in varied ways. The fact that there are various conflicting Christian eschatological (study of last day events) schools of thought, such as, preterism (prophecies were fulfilled in the past), historicism (prophecies are fulfilled throughout history), futurism (prophecies are fulfilled only in the future), and idealism (prophecies merely symbolize spiritual principles) tells us that there's no divinely intended fulfillment, except for mythical assumptions.

Aside from the major prophetic schools of thought, there are also varied and conflicting theories about the 1000-year prophecy, such as pre-millennialism (Christians will be taken to Heaven before tribulations on

Earth); mid-millennialism (Christians will be taken to Heaven during the tribulation), post-millennialism (Christians will be taken to Heaven after the tribulation), and a-millennialism (no literal 1000 years, it's just symbolic).

So whose Bible, and whose interpretation of the Bible, is true and approved by God? Those who would like to be serious students of the Bible, wanting to know God's will for the future of Earth, should be prepared for either sectarian ideological brainwashing or intellectual degradation, if not insanity. If we think of religiously-based moral views, the *Analects* of Confucius (that teaches responsible reciprocation and social respect), the *Tao Te Ching* of Lao Tzu (that teaches humans to live a harmonious life with nature), and Buddhist texts (that teach compassion), offer even better social, ecological, and humane values than the Bible.

14
Heaven and the Primitive Worldview

If Heaven is real, why doesn't Jesus just bring all his believers there now? Why wait till they die, or when the world ends? I bet billionaire Christians would not trade life in Heaven for their luxurious and comfy lives on Earth.

And why did Jesus let hundreds of thousands of his believers die painful deaths during the persecution of the early Christians instead of taking them to Heaven? Church Fathers (like Tertullian, who declared, "... the blood of martyrs is the seed of the Church.") and even present day theologians contend that, had it not been for their persecution, Christianity could have not grown. That's both a sadistic and dumb interpretation of history. It also contradicts the concept that God is loving and responsible. It portrays God as needing horrendous bloodshed so his cause can advance.

But imagine if the Heaven Jesus promised was true. Imagine seeing the disciples of Jesus and a crowd of other believers ascending to Heaven with Jesus. Geez! The whole Roman Empire would have converted within a day. Christian faith could have spread super fast. The whole of humanity today could be in Heaven—except for a few cuckoos who would rather choose Hell. So the world could have been saved long ago. And life now could have been very good.

According to Christian beliefs, Jesus refuses to transport believers to Heaven now. He still wants them to suffer and die first before going to Heaven. So, Hell first, before Heaven. But what's the Christian Heaven, or paradise, anyway?

The Old Testament paradise will actually be an earthly kingdom, a global community with Jerusalem as the religious-political center, a global superpower that will make US or China look like midgets. The New Testament paradise, however, is a hybrid of the mystical world and the material Earth. The details vary among Christian denominational teachings.

Generally, paradise is Earth radically transformed by extreme global catastrophe, a combination of mega earthquakes, war, and even fire from Heaven sent by the Creator-God. After that total annihilation, the New Heaven and New Earth will emerge (Revelation 21). That's quite a show, though a waste of time and resources. Why can't God just voice-activate a New Earth without lots of hassles and horrors that don't make sense? The biblical writers were not that great in making sensible and exhilarating plots. In the New Earth there will be no more sickness, death, and pain. Assimilating the Old Testament paradise, the awesome extraterrestrially-refurbished Jerusalem will be made the global capital.

The Catholic Heaven, though, seems to be more extraterrestrial. It's a paradise above (somewhere in the sky), with a purgatory in the middle (a holding place added on, because God couldn't figure out if others are good or bad), and Hell below. This is much like the ancient worldview of a three tier universe, in an age before telescopes and seismographs were invented. Modern humans, of course, know that there is really no such thing as up, down, or middle in the vastness of the universe—it's just the immense span of space. Although, indeed, the Earth's core is a lot like Hell.

Similarly, the ancient Greeks believed in Elysium (a paradise where heroes become immortals), the Asphodel Meadows (for the indecisive), and Tartarus (a deep abyss of lava for the wicked) ruled by Hades (the root word for Hell). The ancient Jewish concept of an afterlife is more humane than that of

Christian. At death, the human souls goes to Sheol where they undergo regeneration, before they finally go to Olam Haba (the World to Come) or the paradise—no eternal damnation in the lake of fire or the abyss of Tartarus. The ancient Egyptian religion, Hinduism, and Buddhism, share the concept of reincarnation that, at least, offers a better hope for eternal existence than Christian beliefs. If Christians took a closer look at the many magnificent artworks in their cathedrals, they would realize that Christian beliefs like Heaven and Hell are not direct messages from God, but carry-overs of previous ancient myths.

Is the promise of Heaven and the threat of Hell in the afterlife real? Believing in the possible existence of Earth-like planets with features more ideal for life than Earth is more viable,[24] and makes more sense, than believing in Heaven and Hell. In fact, NASA has already confirmed 1700 new planets outside our solar systems.[25] Could there be planets more harsh than Earth? Of course. Is there a lake of lava beneath the Earth? Truly. But to think of these harsh places as a venue for punishing people who don't accept Christian faith is just idiotic!

Christianity could make more sense if it focused on helping make our world a better place to live, rather than obsessing over a mythical Heaven and punishing others with a horrible Hell. Economically empowering the poor, promoting social equality (including gender status), medical access (to help cure many of the diseases), technological/scientific advancements, and, passionately restoring the Earth to a Garden of Eden, are more heavenly and divine. Imagine the billions of dollars and countless of volunteer hours wasted on propagating repressive myths. What if those resources had been utilized on noteworthy causes? Our civilization could have advanced more than now.

To be human is divine. To be earthly is heavenly. To be so heavenly-minded so as to neglect life on Earth will eventually bring Hell to Earth. To shape life on Earth into a paradise, bring Heaven to the world. Nothing complicated, just common sense.

15
God, Patriarchs, and Myths

Why does God have to be male? Can he not be female also? Or even sexless?

If Christians insist that God is male, of course they should also accept that he has male sexual organs; has sexual urges to women, considering he is straight; has the capability to mate and procreate; and has a beard (no problem, many believers think so). If he doesn't cut his hair like the Sikhs, he must have very long hair, considering he's existed for all eternity. He must have eyes that see, a mouth that talks, and also eats, a stomach where his food is digested, and probably has gas every now and then (stressed by the stupidity of his followers), including a rectum, where his waste goes through (smoothly, if he takes fiber). He must also pee (guess what's the color).

But that's too human a characterization of God. And if that's too human, why characterize God as human? If God is not human, why characterize him as exclusively male? Why do Christians feel it's offensive to God, who is not human, to be called female? Is it because Christians have been conditioned to think of God according to its long and deeply embedded patriarchal chauvinism?

How do other religions think of God? Of course, Judaism (where Christians took the Old Testament from, including many of its cultural traditions) and Islam (who carried over and revised the religious traditions of Judaism and Christianity) have a strictly patriarchal God. Hinduism, however, has an abstract and a more mysterious God, or Brahma, that's beyond human reality and understanding. To make it more accessible to humans, Hinduism portrays it in more than 300 million male, female, and even freaky (part human, part animal) gods. At least that's a more gender—and also animal—equitable deity. Shinto has very admirably gender-equitable gods of male and female. In fact, the major god is the female Amaterasu, a sun goddess.

Taoism does not have a personal God, but the *Tao* is regarded as the underlying principle of universal existence that is a synthesis of male and female life principles. Taoism is the most harmonious and unifying of all religions. Confucianism is basically a social philosophy, although traditional Chinese worship various gods and goddesses. Buddhism has no god, although Buddha and Bodhisattvas can help devotees achieve a state of Enlightenment. The ancient Greeks did not only have male and female deities, but even couples, as did the Romans in replicating the Greek deities, aside from their imperial cult that deified both the emperor and his family.

So, except for what academia calls Western religions (Judaism, Christianity, and Islam, that really aren't Western, but Middle Eastern), God is always gender inclusive. But why is the Christian God male? Did God say he is male? And straight, at that? Or is Christianity just chauvinistic? The concept of a strictly male Christian God is rooted in the Christian patriarchs' propensity, not only to subjugate and suppress women, but also to regard women as men's properties. Faithful Christians always emphasize that wives should be subservient to their husbands.

Further complicating the issue of a strictly male God is the concept that God is three beings in one. Trinitarian Christians (including Catholics) believe the one God is: God the Father, God the Son, and God the Holy Spirit. But still no female, despite the fact that Catholics worship Mary as the mother of God. It could have been cool to have God the Mother, God the Son, and the neuter Holy Spirit. Ironically, the Holy Spirit is regarded as neuter, yet the pronoun Christians attribute to the Holy Spirit is still 'he.' So, an all male God, a supreme chauvinist patriarch of the universe.

Could there ever be a female Christian God? I doubt it. Even ordination of women in the sacred ministry is still gender discriminative among many churches, including, of course, the Catholics and the Anglicans. The Lutherans, or the reformers, are still squabbling among themselves to see if indeed women are as divine as men. Hundreds of years of so-called theological scholarship has still not unveiled the dumbness of regarding women as less divine than men. The secular world is more divine than churches in recognizing the equality of men and women.

Let's take a scenario. Imagine the companies in *Forbes*' Best Place to Work mandating that since God could not be female, so there could never be women executives because it's sacrilegious. I bet the mass media and the government would step in and intervene. Why? Because it's blatant gender discrimination. But church patriarchs argue that the church is not the same as the secular corporate world. And in religion women are less dignified than men, if not vile. Ridiculous!

But why no intervention in the church workplace? Because of separation of church and state? Okay, so the church, or any religion, can intervene in the affairs of the state, but the government cannot intervene in the affairs of the church. Remember in the Medieval Ages, when the Church was able to trick people into believing it was above any Earthly kingdom? That trickery is now an essential part of what we call religious freedom—the freedom of the Church to transcend any government. It's a carryover of the Papal Roman tradition that regards the church as transcending government authority, thus being untouchable.

Okay, let's shift to the topic of Jesus the God. If Jesus was a historical Jewish person, with brothers and sisters, and living among the people, he would have been stigmatized for not getting married. Judaism teaches that a man's humanity is complete only in his married state. That's why the creation narrative emphasizes the creation of both man and woman, and the marriage that sacredly bonded them. So, indeed, a celibate, more so a celibate God, is less human and less divine.

No wonder the Jews and the Romans wanted Jesus to be crucified. For the Jews, for a human, more so a celibate human, to claim to be God incarnate is a serious blasphemy against God, deserving the death penalty. For the Romans, for Jewish subjects to claim that Jesus is the Son of God, and the king of a coming kingdom, is plain treason—again, deserving the death penalty. There was only one king-God, Caesar, and one divine kingdom, the Roman Empire. Even today we still see blasphemy of God (as in Muslim countries) and treason (as in North Korea) incurring capital punishment.

Consequently, Jesus was crucified not because he was offering his body as a sacrifice for the sins of humanity. The Romans, despite their cruel gladiator shows and death penalty, found human sacrifice both disgusting and uncivilized. But because he was regarded as a criminal according to both Jewish (religious-political) and Roman (civil) laws.

Furthermore, messianic movements were common a-mong the Jews under the Roman regime, during Jesus' time. Not only Jesus claimed to be the Messiah. There were still other contemporaries, like Simon of Peraea (a former slave of Herod the Great), Athronges (a shepherd like David), and Judas of Gamala, among others. Messiahs were those wanting to lead the liberation of the Jews from the Romans.

And during Jesus' time (again, considering he's an actual historical person), there were also miracle workers. Some were like

Benny Hinn, claiming to heal the sick. Others were more like David Copperfield (except for David's absence of divinity-claim), doing magic shows to astound people. Examples of the many miracle workers were Honi the Circle-Drawer, who brought rain from Heaven; Hanina ben Dosa, who healed the sick; Apollonius of Tyana, who was both a philosopher and a prophet; and even Emperor Vespasian, who healed a blind man and another who was lame.

Those guys must have learned magic tricks from ancient India, if not Egypt. If David Copperfield and Criss Angel were present during Jesus' time, the disciples' loyalty would have easily been split into three. And if Benny Hinn came with his private jet (imagine a healer coming from the heavens with thunder and a blaze of fire from his iron chariot), or probably a helicopter (more like a God descending on a chariot of spinning wheels like Elijah), he could have easily outdone Jesus' divinity. So these days we could have God the Hinn.

So what's the point in all these? Essentially, just an amusing way of saying let's be free from the enslavement of silly myths. It's been a couple of thousands of years now, and there are still more than a billion of us who remain slaves to mythical delusions.

Is it a matter of faith that one believes Jesus as God? No, it's a matter of deeply-ingrained delusions that have coagulated in the psyche of Christians due to a long tradition of dogged, and at times, enforced, indoctrination (brainwashing) that prevents believers from waking to their sensibilities. If Jesus and Christianity are salvific and divine, why punish billions of people (past, present, and future), in the lake of eternal fire for having an outlook in life different from the dizzying breeds of Christian notions? Canadians might ask, "No freedom of thought, eh?" I like that Canadian "eh?" that expresses surprise, while also challenging one to think.

16
Jesus Christ and Other Gods

Why was Jesus deified? Because of the account of his resurrection and miracles?

But claims of miracle healing were common before, during, and after Jesus' time. Even in our medically advanced society, there are still a lot of people claiming to be miracle healers. Of course we know that magic is just an illusion. And if Jesus could feed the five thousand from a few pieces of bread and fish, he could have also fed all peoples of the world in his time. There were still millions of hungry kids in his time, from within Jerusalem to the rest of the Roman Empire, Africa, India, China, and other parts of the world. If God was just feeding a select group, that's unfair to the rest of the hungry world, who were equally God's children.

To use a miracle account as the basis for worshipping a human as the God of the universe does not make sense. The Catholics could have also deified those canonized as saints after confirming their miracles.

What about resurrection? The ancient Egyptian and Canaanite religions had references to dying and rising gods like Osiris and Baal. Greek mythology also mentions humans who died and were resurrected as gods, like Asclepius, who was killed by Zeus but was resurrected and became the god of medicine and healing. Achilles and Heracles, among others, were resurrected into immortality. The Roman founder, Romulus, is claimed to have been resurrected into immortality also.

Justin Martyr, one of the famed Church Fathers (c. 100 to 165 CE) pointed out, "When we say ... Jesus Christ, our teacher, was crucified and died, and rose again, and ascended into Heaven, we propose nothing different from what you believe regarding those whom you consider sons of Zeus (*First Apology* 21)." So, belief in resurrection was not original to Jesus. Nor an original Christian idea. It was adopted from other previous or existing myths. If resurrection is the key to worshipping Jesus as the God of the universe, we should as well worship the rest in other mythologies who also claimed resurrection.

Of course, Christian apologists would say that in Jesus' case there were witnesses. However, many scholars today agree that the passages about Jesus' resurrection in Mark, the earliest among the Gospel writings, were added comments of the scribes, and not part of the original manuscript. So why the absence of the resurrection account of Jesus in the earliest of the Gospel narratives, when it's the foundation of faith in Jesus as God?

Moreover, if Jesus were resurrected, even by today's worldview, his resurrection would have been phenomenal, more so seeing that it was followed by his ascension to Heaven. That phenomenal event would have overwhelmed not just his few followers, but also the Jews, the Romans, the Greeks, the whole Roman Empire and beyond. The news would have spread quickly. The emotional and spiritual impact of the resurrection and ascension to Heaven would have transcended ethnic identities, religious affiliations, and geography, immediately causing an overwhelming empire-wide conversion to Jesus. In this case, even a Caesar would not help but pay homage to Jesus.

However, as stated by Burton L. Mack (a now retired respected scholar of religion and New Testament literature) in his book *Who Wrote The New Testament?* Jesus was mythologized. Instead of focusing on the value of Jesus' teachings, the early New Testament writers began writing myths about Jesus that included, above all, his deification. Later, the church finally institutionalized the belief that Jesus was God, and to solve the problem of having one God (so maintaining Jewish monotheism), while not appearing polytheist (like the Romans and the Greeks), they adopted the concept of the Trinity.

The worship of Jesus as God brought predicaments.

First.

It means that while humanity has had a savior-god since late 30 CE, it also implies that there was no savior-god before that time. Thus no actual salvation for humanity from late 30 CE backward. From Adam and Eve, to Abraham and Moses, among other holy people, there was no actual salvation for them.

Theologians contend that salvation in the Old Testament was prophetic, for salvation pointed to the coming Jesus. However, clearly the Old Testament people of God worshipped the God other than Jesus. And certainly, as I mentioned earlier, they would not only reject worshipping either an incarnate God or a deified human, but also detest it as blasphemy against their God. Here, Christianity contradicts itself.

Second.

Because Jesus the God came a couple of thousand years ago now, it means that we now have the grand, gracious, caring, omniscient, omnipotent, omnipresent Chairman-CEO of the universe. It means that, at last, after billions of years of evolution, we finally have the reliable and efficient God who can manage humanity (including how big a population we shall get), human life (who will die in tragedies or not, including who will win the lotto), and the universe (like where the asteroid will fall, where an earthquake will strike—he must have hated Japan) in the fullness of divine love and grace.

And where was he when thousands of his believers were burned at the stake by Nero? Where was he when hundreds of thousands died fighting one another while competing for the exclusive rights to the Heaven he offered? Where was he when millions (men, women, and children alike), died horribly throughout history because of greed and hatred for one another? What about the millions of emaciated skeleton-like precious human beings—adults, babies, and toddlers—dying because of hunger, poverty, and human cruelties?

Christian theologians boldly declare that God is omnipresent—so he's present everywhere, witnessing all those human miseries.

But Christian apologists, of course, always attempt to vindicate the God they worship. But why vindicate God, if he is God, omniscient and omnipotent? The bottom line is, and common sense tells us, there is no Jesus the God graciously caring for humanity and managing the universe—no Creator determining where the asteroids will hit, which stars will die, where black holes will emerge, or where the mega-floods and super typhoons, or high intensity earthquakes and massive famines will hit.

Theologians would argue that the occurrence of dreadful disasters without God's intervention is all part of the divine mystery. That's nonsense. So, because of God's preoccupation with keeping himself mysterious, he did not mind letting countless of his beloved human creatures suffer miserable deaths? That's a humongous waste of sacred lives for a petty hobby. Don't tell me we cannot explain everything so we'll just take it by faith. That's nonsense too. Because it would mean that Jesus is a very aloof God and a really stupid manager of the universe.

Imagine a corporate CEO doing nothing while his company is crumbling down. Or a fire chief doing nothing while a building across from the fire hall is burning. Or a chief of police just watching crime happening across the police station. Or a president, or prime minister, enjoying a luxurious vacation while his country is in a grave state of emergency. That's ridiculously insane.

In essence, there's really no difference between the worship of Jesus (and other Gods and Goddesses of world religions) and the deities of ancient mythology. They are all mythical objects of devotion created by humans as a catharsis for the pressures of everyday life and insurmountable realities. Accepting our limitations and becoming creatures-creators, can bring more bliss to our lives than obsessing over infinity and omnipotence.

Yes, our psyches yearn for a superhero figure to whom we can anchor our hopes amid uncertainties. That's why superhero movies thrive. We know they're not real, we know their actions are all in green screen. We know the good guy wins in the end, and the bad guy loses. But we still enjoy watching it. We enjoy the drama, it entertains our souls and releases the stress from the humdrums of everyday life. Problems arise, though, when we become obsessed with superheroes, forgetting that to be human is divine.

17
New Birth and Hallucination

Want to be sure of paradise? Then be born again, say the Christians. For no one can enter paradise unless he or she is born again first (John 3:2-4). Spiritual rebirth for Christians is a must for assuring believers of Heaven in the afterlife. But what does being born again, or regeneration (a seemingly high sounding theological word borrowed from biology), mean?

First.

The easiest to understand is the Catholic way. When an infant is baptized (the rite of pouring water over a baby's head, similar to a shampooing in a salon) by a priest, the supernatural life of God (or Jesus) is infused (like infusing a tea) in the child. Bingo! The child has now been reborn (the word reminds me of Johnny English) spiritually.

An infant, who by law (I'm pretty sure it's worldwide) is not yet morally liable for his or her acts, is now made righteous. Except perhaps for the poop in the diaper, I don't really see anything wicked in an infant. So, now, seconds (not sure if it takes minutes, hours, days, or, whatnot) after the baptism, the infant is ready to enter the kingdom of God.

That's eerie though, for the paradise is in the afterlife. All I want to see, and foresee, in an infant is laughter, joy, and a wonderful life ahead. Not the expectation of the forthcoming afterlife.

But, on a more positive side, now that the infant is baptized and infused with the supernatural life of God. But does this mean the infant has become supernatural? You know, the inviolable cause and effect rule of nature? Supernatural life effects supernatural living. With great power comes great reflexes. Now that the infant is godlike, will it never be mundane again?

And forever righteous? Growing up till adulthood with no drugs, no crime, no child pornography, or pedophilia (as seen on TV among the reborn priests), ever? Or is baptism like charging a battery: the infant, after growing older, needs recharging of God's life again? I thought God's life, or energy, lasted for eternity.

There's something scary though. Parents, instead of getting excited for their child's divinity, should instead be fearful that the propensity of pedophile priests, including those grooming to be priests, might infect their kids' fragile and innocent souls.

Second.

Let's talk about the more complicated view of rebirth, the Protestant view. First, you need to be indoctrinated and believe with all your heart that the ideas being taught to you are the only truth, and nothing else but the truth. So what is this truth? Of course, it is learning doctrines, or being indoctrinated—in other words, brainwashing. After indoctrination (brainwashing, interrupts a minion of Despicable Me), one believes that he or she is now closer to God because of the new ideas learned.

The next thing is proving one's loyalty to the new teachings, or religious ideology, directly equated as loyalty to the church and God. After regularly attending church services, one has proven themselves worthy of the grand paradise-entrance rite, baptism. Some cry, others are nervous. I hope no one is excited to enter the paradise very soon. Then down one goes into the watery grave and comes out a new person, reborn to a life in Jesus. Drama lingers for a while, then dissipates.

Then, when the once newly baptized becomes an active member of the church, or even a pastor, he, or she, will have learned to live amid the worldly politicking, financial exploitation, manipulation of people's conscience, sectarian conflicts, dogmatism, and, in some cases, even martyrdom complexes (willingness to sacrifice and, even die for the sake of a religious notion) of fellow born again Christians.

I thought the power of Jesus to make one righteous, being the power of an omnipotent God, lasted for a lifetime. Even in our age of the rechargeable, which might accept a Green Lantern needing recharging, would still think of a rechargeable divinity as silly.

Third.

The Pentecostal way. It's the Protestant way plus, to make it more mystical, speaking in tongues. Speaking in tongues is regarded as the sign of the baptism of the Holy Spirit. One can just mumble his or her way to Heaven. Other enterprising church members even offer to interpret the mumbling speech. No embarrassment for the interpreter though (unlike the interpreter at Mandela's funeral), because he or she can say anything and the congregation will just say, "Amen!"

Thus, Pentecostal baptism is not just one but two baptisms: water and Spirit. Many of the controversial (or to put it candidly, morally questionable) pastors nowadays have this two-tier baptism. The Holy Spirit failed to transform Pat Robertson's bigotry; he still declared that the Haiti earthquake and Hurricane Katrina were sent by God. The Holy Spirit was not able to overpower Jimmy Swaggart's lust for escorts, nor Jim Bakker's propensity for fraud (others add extra-marital affairs too). Or Creflo Dollar's appetite for lavishness (the lifestyle that even Pope Francis abhors).

Examples are long, and the fact is clear: there's no clinical evidence to prove that church baptism cures one's psychosis. For sure, the coolness of church water, particularly in the summer, is relaxing. But a spa treatment might be more therapeutic to the soul than baptism.

The enigma of spiritual rebirth.

But what does being born again really mean? For believers, it means that their old lives are gone, and new righteous lives in Jesus have begun. Jesus now makes them righteous. But they are still imperfect, courtesy of a faulty Jesus process, and so relapse to old life is included. When the momentary sense of moral grandeur subsides, believers who are hateful now uses God to hate others.

If those born again are still imperfect, there's really no difference between imperfect decent secular people and Christians. If those born again are already perfect, then they could have been holier than the Pope or the Dalia Lama, or Warren Buffet and Bill Gates, who remain unscathed by accusations of unethical practices, in sharp contrast to a number of born again celebrity pastors. If Buffet and Bill Gates were like the megachurch pastors, imagine the scale of money they'd bilk from investors.

The world is full of non-Christians and secular people who have not been baptized, in any form, by the church, but who live decent moral lives, and contribute to the betterment of humanity more than Christians. Righteousness is not the exclusive domain of the church, or any religion. Righteousness is a sense common among people wanting to live normal decent lives.

What Christians really mean by spiritual rebirth, or living a righteous life that would qualify them for Heaven, is nothing but a combination of these trivia:

One.

A mystical feeling that they are righteous. The feeling is induced by the dramatic effect of church ritual, creating a fleeting mystical ambiance of oneness with God. This mystical feeling is also accompanied by a compulsion to live according to denominational deportment. After a short while the mystical feeling subsides. The newborn Christian is now focused on sectarian behavior, reinforced by a delusion of moral grandeur. It's this delusion of moral grandeur that Christians equate as righteousness, not present in our common world that they call sinful.

Two.

Assuming holiness, because their pastors preach that those who profess Jesus as savior, and are faithful church members, are righteous and Heaven-bound. It's a sort of theoretical righteousness, a theory that all those who profess to be God's people are righteous. Ironically, believers claim righteousness in contrast not only to the secular, but also to those belonging to other denominations.

Three.

Spiritual rebirth by virtue of new denominational affiliation. This is a very common delusion among Christians. Other Christians still call outside churches 'satanic.' Most would regard themselves holier than others.

In fact, when a church member is seen attending other churches, more so a clergy preaching in a different church, church members and church bureaucracy tag such acts as heresy, and thus wicked.

Four.

A sense of holiness resulting from doctrinal adherence. Doctrinal adherence cements the believer's sense of holiness. This hallucination of holiness becomes deeply embedded in the believer's psyche. That questioning, or worse, denying the truthfulness of church doctrines, is believed to cause one's forfeiture of Heaven, and sure destiny to Hell.

Five.

Living a sectarian way of life—as silly as avoiding pork chops, or wearing a monotonous dress style (although at times it may look cool). Or a more ritualistic life, like not missing the tiny wafer and wine (don't know what makes a little wine holy). Or a behavioral one like always respecting the holy priests (though they may undress you).

The more institutional ones, like don't forget to pay your monthly tithes and weekly offerings. Clergies need that badly, more than the Heaven they promise.

And of course attending church regularly. Otherwise, one will miss the blessings of God. If God's blessings reside in the church, he could have saved churches from being vandalized by wicked humans, or destroyed by acts of nature (also tagged acts of God).

Think through.

There is no life more sublime than a life of inclusive goodness. On the contrary, the life of exclusive goodness propagated by the church is not only a selfie intended to brag one's moral glamour, but also a rich source of bigotry and judgementalism.

A good person doesn't need to be baptized if he or she is truly good. Neither does a bad person. There's no scientific studies supporting the claim that baptism will transform a vile person into a good one. Changes in a person's lifestyle and outlook can happen in many avenues, even in unexpected places like bars, after pouring it out to a friend. Or movies, after watching a life-changing film. Or secular motivational workshops. Military, and martial arts training also change people from someone lax to someone disciplined.

Changes in one's life through religion are not exclusive to one faith, but a common experience across religions. The only difference is the resulting form of religious lifestyle, because of different beliefs, are loaded with all sorts of varying theories.

However, a life shaped by religious ideology is a dogged life full of ideological expectations and bigotries. There's nothing more liberating for one's soul than a life free from ideological constraints. Regenerative life is not about patronizing religious theory, it's about creative living that contributes to the common goodness of everyday human life.

Making Sense out of it All

18
Why the Doggedness of Faith?

Why the doggedness of faith? Why do believers persevere in their beliefs even when it means losing their sacred lives? From the martyrdom of ancient Christians in the Roman Empire, to death and sufferings in religious wars, to committing mass suicide—we see believers persisting in and trading their lives and families for mere religious ideas that do not make sense at all.

Reflecting on my journey, I uncovered these core causes of religious madness.

One.

Believers, through continuous indoctrination, have lost their common sense. In fact, using common sense, for adherents, is offensive to God, and will lead them to Hell. The only option they have is to follow the teachings of their church. The intensity of blind faith is even deeper in cults because of the charisma and skillful control of their leaders.

Of course, common sense is an innate human quality. But common sense, in believers' psyches, is clouded by an overlaying church delusion, plus the refusal to use common sense because of fears. Namely, the fear of divine curses, fear of the hostile world outside the church, and fear of receiving a stigma that would result in losing the church's fellowship. It should be noted that, for believers, the only support group they feel they have is their church group.

Covering a believer's common sense are the five layers of blind faith: induced church delusion, willful refusal to be awakened to reality, congregationally-rooted fear of God's curse, personal fear of losing a life-support group, and fear of the assumed hostile world outside. Despite the fact that, aside from their weekend church service, during the weekdays they live in a secular world like normal people. But their consciousness of church affiliation makes them believe they're protected from the evils of the world, and when they backslide, that protection will be withdrawn by God, and they will be subject to all sorts of tragedies in life. That's the slavery of religiously-induced fear.

It takes extraordinary courage for church adherents to break free from the shackles of church myth. But those who do dare, will realize that the secular world is much larger than their narrow myth-driven world, and offers them the freedom to creatively realize their humanity.

Imagine humans living in deep caves for quite a time—believing that the world outside is hostile. In 1974, Hiroo Onoda, a World War II Japanese intelligence officer, made sensational headlines. When WWII ended, Hiroo was lost and stranded in a jungle in the Philippines. For years he survived and lived in a secluded world as a faithful soldier of Japan's Sun-God emperor. Believing he was fighting a war of divine and noble cause, his loyalty to his Emperor-God was undying. Despite some efforts, he refused to accept the reality that the war had ended, until his former commanding officer convinced him that the war was long over, and there was a new world outside the jungle. When he finally surrendered, brave soldier as he was, he was shaken to see the new world. He could not believe the war was over. He even found it hard to adapt to the new life in his beloved country[26].

Accepting new realities beyond one's devotion to sacred myths isn't easy. Living for quite a time amid the darkness of church myth, and exclusion from the wider world, results in a distorted view of human life and existence. Believers tremble at the thought of leaving the church and the God they worshipped. But those who dare leave, realize that life outside their ideological prison cell is more beautiful and grander.

Two.

The affinity to hope for something, though it may not come true. It's the same hope that drives millions and millions of people throughout the world to buy lotto tickets, hoping they'll get lucky, despite also knowing that their chance is slim. However, in lotto, people know that the jackpot money is there. In religion, no one has seen Heaven at all, so the chance of winning the grand prize in lotto is much more reasonable than the chance of making it to paradise in the afterlife.

But why do believers stick to their false hopes? One of their usual arguments (the Pascal's Wager) is that they have nothing to lose if Heaven is not real, but non-believers have everything to lose should Heaven be true. That's not true though, for believers lose their time, money, and efforts for their fantasy, and also forfeit participation in freeing humans from any form of slavery, including slavery to religious ideology.

Imagine if the church, from the Medieval Ages until now, had achieved an overwhelming success in controlling the world. Advancement in chemistry (tagged by ancient faithful Christians as satanic), medicines (imagine regarding disease as caused by God's curse, if not by witches), and other facets of human science and technology, could have not been realized because of being suppressed by religious myths. Even governments today could still be directly under the sovereignty and exploitation of scheming and malicious clergies.

Hope for a more advanced civilization, and much better quality of human life, is bleak in religion. Yes, others say, Christians make life better in many Third World countries through their humanitarian efforts. But so do secular foundations like the Bill & Melinda Gates Foundation, the global UNICEF, the Rotary Club, City Harvest, and Greenpeace among others, without the guise of religious evangelism. There are a wide range of secular institutions bringing hope to humanity in the many aspects of our human life: from medicine to engineering and technological advancement, to entrepreneurship, education and research, and even space exploration.

Hope without the pretense of mythical paradise and fear of Hell brings an even more creative and useful driving force in the shaping of a more truly hopeful world.

Three.

The dread of accepting fresh realities that will result in letting go of deeply rooted traditions. The aforementioned story of Hiroo shows how people with sacral conviction would sacrifice their lives refusing to believe reality. Likewise, believers in the so-called religious cults; although no different (except, in the degree of their lunacy) than believers in commonly accepted churches—sacrifice their lives in refusing to see the world as it is.

Even in globally respected centers of education, we still find academicians who believe that science should be directed by religious beliefs, ignoring the fact that scientific advancement enhances our ability to learn more about the realities of nature and our universe beyond the confinements of religious myths. An example is the notion of Intelligent Design, that not only distorts science, but also praises ancient biblical myths that were, in fact, adopted from other earlier cultural myths, as the foundation of science.

Imagine a patient in a life and death situation being brought to an ER of a modern hospital, and the doctor first reads spells from the ancient Egyptian Book of the Dead so the person's soul will be assured safe journey into the next realm. That's outrageous! But the fact is, even in our technologically advanced civilization, religion still plays a dominant role in many aspects of life, from medical to social ethics, politics, mass media norms, and even films.

Religious traditions have taken deep root in our civilization. Many in our society today still assume there can be no ethics, or morality, or even hope, beyond religion. Ignoring that ethics, morality, and hope for our future can be more clearly discerned without the prejudices and biases of gender discriminating, ethnocentric, and myth-driven religious assumptions.

Fourth.

Social pressure. This includes family pressure (the influence of religious family members), peer pressure (pressure from religious friends), and societal pressure (the stigma society imposes on atheists, agnostics, humanists).

A member of a religious family wanting to be free from religion is usually tagged as a black sheep. And is tagged so despite one's esteemed morality. More so with a church member leaving the fold, who would be regarded not just as a black sheep, or a backslider, but as falling into the devil's hands, and thus sinful, in a sense now part of the devil's kingdom.

Ironically, even a number of governments today still favor religion more than secularism. There is always a natural propensity for governments to please the religious while eschewing secular populations. An exception was the previous minority government of Quebec that launched the Quebec Charter of Values in 2013, restricting public sector employees from wearing or displaying conspicuous religious symbols. Years back, Quebec was under the clout of the Catholic Church. Then it tried to set an example of breaking free from religious constraints.

Many urban Quebecers supported it, while major political parties and even provinces like Ontario (where Catholic schools are still publicly funded while other religious schools are not) expressed opposition against it. Those who were against the Charter invoked religious freedom, ignoring the fact that religious freedom also means the freedom of the secular state from religious-political control. Religious freedom does not mean that the religious are wantonly free to impose their varied and conflicting beliefs on the government and on all aspects of society.

It's the nature of religion to control human will and dominate human life. We see this not only among ancient societies, but even in our modern civilization, among Middle Eastern, Western, Oriental, and African countries. Any form of pressure exerted to preserve the dominance of religion in our everyday life would not only perpetuate the cycle of religious dogmatism, but would also prevent people from exploring humanizing alternative value systems.

Fifth.

The fear of God. Contrary to popular belief that believers commit their lives and resources to the church because of their love of God, they do so because of their fear of God.

Fear that should they not continue to worship their sectarian God, they will lose their fantasized Heaven in the afterlife and be punished in eternal Hell. Fear that should they fail to give tithes and offerings, God will withdraw his protection over them. Their businesses will suffer losses. They will lose their jobs. They will suffer bankruptcy. Or worse, tragedy will befall them. That's where religion thrives. It exploits human fear, and offers people a cathartic hallucination in exchange for their money and a lifetime of resolute social support.

Think it through.

It's only by facing our fears of the unknown that we can know the nature of the unknown. It's only by freeing ourselves from the delusion of myths that we can appreciate much of the realism of life. The tantrums and conflicts of the gods should teach us to disdain being driven by sacral destructive forces. For the fulfillment of our humanity, we need to nurture, and make use of, our innate and divine creativity and constructive penchant.

19
Candid Soul Searching

Soul searching is the gateway to a new path. How I became religious, particularly Christian, might be providential, but what followed after was truly divine, to say it in Christian lingo.

I was born to a poor family, but every year my dad made sure I got the best dress on Holy Week. Nothing was more special for my dad than the Holy Week because, for him, it was the time to remember that Jesus died to save us. I guess it was his way of ensuring that his family, who did not have enough on Earth, could be assured of a much better life in the hereafter. And at least he could be assured that we still had God on our side to take care of us and help us make it through another meal, every day.

So I grew up believing that when all other things fail, God is my only remaining hope. I cherished that heritage of faith from my dad. I did not question the existence of God. I also accepted as truth whatever the priest would say. I believed that God was not only spiritually, but also literally, present in the church.

When it was time for me to take my Communion, I would approach the altar with awe and reverence, believing it a very holy place where God was. I felt the bread and wine lifted me to a celestial sphere where I could feel the presence of angels around me. I wouldn't even dare touch the Bible, I just intently stared at it, while feeling the heavenly ambience that surrounded so sacred a Word of God. The sculptures of saints all around the church would mesmerize me. And at times I would whisper, "Please help my dad find money so we'll always have food on the table." I would serenely smile, trusting the saints would answer my prayer, and make my dad happy.

My dad's periodic spirituality so impacted my life that when I was in pre-school I decided to attend a convent. So religion has a long rootedness in my life and my outlook on human existence. That early influence made me decide to serve my dad's object of devotion. I dreamt of becoming a holy man someday so I could bring God's blessings to the poor, like my dad and our family. Nothing is more pleasing to God than someone who dedicates his life to him, I thought. And nothing is holier on Earth than the church. Although in high-school I changed my dream-career, but serving God caught up with again me afterwards.

To make the long story short, I became a clergyman and a theologian focused on serving God and saving humanity. For some time my passion for the ministry seemed to never cease. Way back then there was still the Cold War, and I had no hardship deciding which ideological camp I should support. I regarded atheism as an enemy of God and the church.

A few years after the Iron Curtain crumbled down, I met a Polish immigrant in a park telling me about the horrors of the Nazis and how he realized there was no God after all. I could sense his emotion and the deepness of his words, but I disdained him for his lack of faith in God. I just could not figure out why people could not see God everywhere. I believed then that no matter what happens in the world, God was always there. I could not explain everything, but he was always there. Mystery was always part of his divinity, so there were things about him that I could not explain, and I just accepted in faith.

But the time came when, little by little, I began to see the realities outside my dogged notions. I encountered accusations against the Church, then struggled whether to quickly dismiss these as the devil's attempts to destroy the holy church of God, or to confront it with an open heart and a critical mind. When I discovered that accusations about sexual abuses by my fellow clergymen were real, I wrestled with my spirit whether to accept forgiveness or call for justice. Is it more just to forgive the erring pedophile servants of God than for victims to be accorded justice?

Though for years I was aware of the realities inside the Church, it never crossed my mind to think critically about it until the day I discovered that erring clergymen, transferred to other parishes, committed the same sins over and over again. I began to see the immoralities, not just inside the Catholic Church, but also among the Protestants, the

Pentecostals, and a number of popular megachurches.

Then I realized that clergymen's lust for luxuries, zeal for political conspiracy, propensity for exploiting conscience, and hypocrisy, made the churches of Christianity no more divine than any other mundane institution. That awakening to perceive, with an open heart and a rational mind, the realities inside the church, also led me to ponder on the foundations of my faith.

Taking a heartfelt look at the issues of the world outside my protected enclave, I began to see the reality of human life and existence with depths I'd never recognized before. I saw thousands of pitiful hungry children dying in hunger everyday in the arms of their emaciated mothers. Meanwhile, in the seat of God's kingdom on Earth, luxuries abounded. And outside the church was a world where the rich—who are becoming even richer—wasted millions of dollars on a long list of petty matters.

I asked myself questions like: Why do inhuman dictators thrive for years, plundering their countries into poverty, while enjoying horrors of genocide? Why do the forces of nature, labeled acts of God, always unleash its power against the deprived, while the greedy privileged always go unscathed? These, and many more questions, profoundly troubled me.

For days I fasted, and wrestled with God for answers, like Jacob wrestling with an angel in the Old Testament story. I talked to colleagues, who did nothing but warn me that my critical thinking was leading me to fall into the hands of the devil. I argued,

"What about those pedophiles, are they not more inclined to the Devil than me?" They would just answer that we were all ordained by God. I only became more restless.

Then I took the courage to confide in a senior mentor, whom I respected for his sincerity and acuity, though he was not really so congenial to me. I poured out my doubts, coupled with my growing critical mindedness. To my surprise, after a couple of hours of private talks, he bid me to follow my heart, to walk according to the light I had discovered, and to pursue what I believed would be more truly divine for humanity.

At this point I was wearing a mask, my conscience bothered. But I had to continue wearing a mask for the sake of those I loved. I could not wait for the time to come when I could finally declare myself free, without hurting, or bringing heartache, to those I loved. I knew, even if they accepted me, that others would stigmatize, if not ostracize, them. But I looked forward to the time when our society was finally ready to accept freedom from the enslavement of religious myth as humanizing rather than degrading. That would be the time when common sense would triumph over fairy tales...

20
Thinking Through

Can religion really make me more human than secularism? Are religious values more noble than secular? Many people assume that there can be no morality outside religion. They regard religion as the repository of moral values, and all the good things that humanity can have. Really?

Okay, what makes me as a religious person, and a Christian in particular, different from secular people, and atheists in particular? Well, I go to church, and I believe in God, of course, because I'm religious.

That's a dumb differentiation though. What about the essence of being human? Okay, I don't steal. I don't commit adultery. I don't murder people. I don't bear false witness against my neighbors. But normal secular people do that also. I don't mean that because others are atheists, or don't go to church, that they are murderers, robbers, and criminals. That's a very irrational, if not insane, characterization of non-religious people.

What about the notion that anti-religious people like Hitler (a Catholic, in fact), Stalin, Mao, or Pol Pot? But it was not atheism, itself, that drove them to commit inhumanity. On the contrary, their obsession and enslavement to myths made them tyrannical zealots. Likewise, with the Christian Crusaders, the perpetrators of the Inquisition, the Conquistadors!

But those were the past. Let's talk about the present and something more personal. I still couldn't figure out the essential difference between religious and secular people. What about people who go to bars and nightclubs to drink and become drunkards? Or people who go to movie theaters. My goodness! Conservative Christians even think movie theaters are evil, while they, and even their pastors, watch the same films in their homes. I don't get it. If it's the place that makes an activity sinful, well, theatres are not brothels, and most are very comfy.

Bars and nightclubs, especially those with exotic dancers, are sleazy for many decent secular people. They don't want to see a president, or prime minister—though they may not be churchgoers—go to these places. But not all secular people go there, and not all secular people are drunkards either. What about the pedophile clergymen in the church? The pastors (both straight and not) who secretly engage in extramarital affairs or who hire escorts? Or the mega-church pastors bilking hard-earned money from their church members? Shall I also avoid going to church because there are sinful people there too?

Being religious does not really guarantee that one will be righteous and moral. Nor does being secular, or atheist, destine one to be wicked and immoral. Besides, values, like human dignity, the sacredness of human life, and justice, among others, are common universal human values. Humanity has a common sense of what's right and wrong, and this ısense is innate in our nature. It's the driving force that shapes our survival as civilized beings. Human beings commit the right or the wrongs acts regardless of whether they are religious or not.

What about hope? Hope is one of the driving forces in human life. Without hope people lose the reason and the will to live. Believers claim that no other institution offers hope more than religion. But hope is not the exclusive domain of religion. Climbers hoping to reach the summit of Everest, athletes hoping to win gold medals at the Olympics, or business people hoping to succeed in their ventures, do not necessarily resort to the church as their source of hope.

Hope is an innate and common driving force embedded in our human psyche, and instead of religion originating hope for humanity, it's humanity hoping for something beyond Earthly life that originated religion. Religion is not really the source of human hope, our psyche is. It's part of our mental processes in coping with our survival and having a meaningful existence. Not all who hoped for something better, and have realized such hope, got their inspiration from the church (in particular) or religion (in general).

The Giving Pledge, a commitment by the world's wealthiest to dedicate their wealth to helping make human life better—giving hope, in a concrete and beneficial way, to the deprived—was pioneered by Bill Gates and Warren Buffet. They did it not because of religious faith (since they are not churchgoers, nor spiritual), but because of our universal human value of the common good. Many of those who pledged were not really churchgoing or religious people, but secular, and more divinely generous and kinder than many mega-church pastors obsessed with worldly luxuries.

Hope for a more dignified and meaningful human life is not exclusive to the religious, or religion. It can come from the secular world as well. In fact, the secular source of hope is even more altruistic, without requiring ideological commitment, as in luring humanitarian recipients to become church members and subscribe to church doctrines. Or requiring a lifetime of idolatry, worshipping a deity to ensure the realization of the things hoped for.

So what really makes churchgoers, or the religious, essentially different from the secular? Really nothing? Most secular normal people are as committed to their families and living a decent moral life as religious people. Of course, Christians would contend that they have no hope of Heaven.

But let's be open-minded and candid about the promise of paradise in the afterlife. *First*, there are more crucial issues in our present life than the afterlife. *Second*, really, the afterlife is a fantasy. And *third*, the offer of Heaven merely creates confusion (of which, among the religious Heaven is true), conflicts (because each church and religion competes among one another for the rights to the fantasized paradise), and draws people away from coping with the realities of everyday life (by simply being obsessed with a mythical world).

Vanity of vanities, as the mythical wise man, Solomon, would say. But imagine how an institution whose major product is a notion of a fantasy world, has succeeded in creating a vast network of wealthy global enterprises, milking people, rich and poor, alike. It's very baffling how our modern society still cowers at the thought of unraveling the exploitive and enslaving nature of religion. Stunted critical thinking, and lack of will to be free and explore what's beyond, coupled by religious protectionism, perpetuate people's addictions to mystical hallucination.

21
Considerations Before Leaving the Church

"What shall you do if you leave the Church?" That question from my senior mentor echoed in my mind.

I was a theologian-clergyman. Secular job places didn't know what to do with people like me. Aside from being wary that I might still bring religion, if not ill will against it, into my work place, my transferable skills were not that much. Yes, I could deliver public presentations, but most likely I would still carry over my preaching style. Yes, I could teach, but what courses? Theology? Yes, I could counsel. But my counseling training was pastoral counseling, and most likely counseling using biblical passages.

After pondering whether to leave the Church or not, I ended up listening to my mentor, who was now becoming a friend. "Just keep it to yourself," he said. He further added these words of wisdom:

"If your reason convinced you to be an atheist, let it be. But continue serving the Church as if you're still a believer. For now, address your struggles for meaning in a fresh way. But do it as a clergyman, a doctor of the soul who may or may not be a believer. In essence, a healer of the soul, though a wounded healer."

So I decided to stay, while making my first ventures into helping liberate others from the same bondage I'd been into for years, and wanting to be free someday.

For those considering to leave the church now, let me share my thoughts.

For Clergymen.

First.

Do you have a viable alternative career and livelihood? The transferable skills and experience of clergymen for secular jobs are very low. Not everyone can be like Dan Barker (an evangelical pastor turned atheist) of the Freedom From Religion Foundation, who has the charisma and connections to raise funds and create a successful and influential career for himself. And despite the fact that evolution is common among the academia, and many scientists and academics are secular, courses on the philosophical foundation of atheism are still rare. So even the possibility of getting a teaching position in atheism is still rare.

If you're a non-Catholic pastor who has a family to raise, where will you get money to make ends meet? How will you ensure the future of your kids? When a family member gets sick and is not covered by government health care, where will you get the money to pay for expensive medical bills? How will you pay for your mortgage, and where will you live?

You may have some sympathetic supporters. But how long will they sustain you? Not for life, most likely. So don't leave the ministry out of impulse. Prepare before you leave by professionally qualifying yourself with an alternative career you love as much as the ministry. Be sure you have the interest, the potential skills for development, and make sure it's a job that's in demand. Otherwise, your fresh vision of liberation from the shackles of religious myth will turn into an economic bondage and a despondent life. Don't jump from one myth to another. Before jumping away from a world of myth, be sure you'll land in a real life of fresh opportunities.

Second.

Can you stay alive being alone without an extensive network of social support? Remember, atheism is an outlook on life that's liberating for many, but religion, particularly Christianity and Islam, is not just a belief, but also a network of institutions. With the network comes the church, schools, hospitals, para-church ministries, and the whole gamut of religious institutional systems with embedded extensive social networks. That's why religion thrives, that's why Christian faith thrives. Because of its extensive networks of social support.

There are now atheist organizations and budding atheist fellowships like The Sunday Assembly, but the fact is, the atheist social support network is still very infantile compared to complex religious institutional systems. Atheistic movements are still primarily focused on propagating the concept. And your closest friends among the clergy will sooner or later push themselves away from you. The atheist movement still has to establish itself as a socially supportive movement.

Third.

Are you ready for the church's holy retribution? No church minister, more so someone regarded as a brilliant theologian and charismatic clergy, could leave the church intact. Your church, either its academia or its parish, is your previous long-term employer. Don't expect the church to give you a good recommendation to your new secular employer. It's a pattern that the church, being a dogmatic institution, will always label those who get free as heretics, lost people, if not rebels. There's nothing positive the church could say to your prospective employers. They profess to have the love of Jesus, but their hidden hatred is as eternal as the Hell it promotes.

Fourth.

Is your family (and if you're a non-

Catholic pastor, your wife and kids), ready to be stigmatized as atheistic by your Christian friends and society as a whole? Can you all cope with the unjust and irrational stigmatization that may linger for some time, until our society (which may still take years) is transformed into a more inclusive and sensible community?

Fifth.

Can you cope with the challenges and trauma of transformation? Being transformed from a longtime believer into a newborn atheist can be traumatic (albeit exhilarating!).

You'll be like Yellow in Trina Paulus' *Hope for the Flowers*. I would imagine the pain and the shock is like seeing yourself transformed into something different, really much different. But, of course, in the end the pain and the shocking experiences will be transcended by the beauty and wonder of a new life. No longer will you be bound by ancient myth, but engulfed by the fresh and blissful purpose of making life more creative and free.

For church members.
First.

Consider the aforementioned need for social support. Social support is a basic consideration for those leaving the church. Of course you can find alternate non-religious social groups in civic organizations like the Rotary or Lion's Club, sports clubs, and other non-profit organizations, where you can have fellowship while also engaging in worthy and enjoyable endeavors.

Second.

Consider what you need to cope with stigmatization and personal transformation. Though it's easier for church members than clergymen to transition from being religious to being secular, becoming secular still poses challenges.

It takes a process to transform from one outlook in life to another. There's also a tendency to relapse, especially in times of crisis. It's usual for the ex-religious to be confronted by the fear of the unknown and uncertainty, and have a propensity to call upon the deity they once worshiped. It's a normal reaction while one is still in the process of finding an alternative anchor for the human psyche. Reading secular motivational books that are more realistic, and guides one to develop courage and the will to be, and to do, is empowering.

As human beings, we all face challenges in life, but remember, countless people have found success and fulfillment in life without resorting to a church or religion. Bertrand Russell (famous philosopher and activist), Noam Chomsky (one of the most notable present-day philosopher), Linus Pauling (one of the most influential chemists in history), James D. Watson (a discoverer of DNA), Andrew Carnegie (famous American industrialist and philanthropist), Peter Higgs (Noble laureate of God particle), David Suzuki (Canadian environmentalist), Sigmund Freud, Charles Darwin, Bruce Lee, Jodie Foster, Steve Jobs, Mark Zuckerberg, and Warren Buffet and Bill Gates (two of the leading productive non-religious philanthropists) are just a few examples of the long list of happy non-religious people. In fact, they have all brought blessings to humanity in their respective fields of endeavors. The School of Life in London also provides secular alternative to religion.

Courage, hope, and the drive to fulfill our dreams are innate human qualities. Even creatures in lower animal kingdom, I suspect, may also possess these qualities in their own level. At times, fantasy adds color to our lives. Often, imagination leads us to create a new world where our humanity advances like never before. But not in a fashion that enslaves us and restricts our constructive creatorship.

Kids enjoy fairy tales. But for mature humans these stories are for kids to inspire their imagination, so when they grow older they can shape their lives into something magical, and realize that the magic of life is the bliss of life lived in the now, not in the hereafter.

22
Why People are Leaving the Church

Leaving the church isn't a trivial matter. For many believers the church has been their second family. And for others, like those with broken families, the church is often their primary family. No question, for most believers, particularly those with a long history in the same church, the church has been their only social support group.

But why are a growing number of Christians leaving the church? There are a number of serious reasons that, at times, even the church itself takes for granted. Let me share some of these major reasons.

First.

Irrelevance. Why are many churches closing? Simple: because people don't find it relevant anymore. And why do megachurches seem to blossom? Because, in the meantime, churchgoers find it an alternative venue for letting off steam from the pressures of everyday life. It's comfy, with entertaining music and motivational talks, and it's emotionally charged, particularly among the Pentecostals, where crying, for men, women, and children alike, are not only acceptable, but stimulated.

So the days are fading when the relevance of the church hinged on its sole authority to send one to Heaven or Hell. What more and more people are looking for are venues to release the stresses of everyday life. That's why singing out loud and church dancing work, as does motivational and fun-filled preaching. That's why charismatic and humorous speakers thrive more than the boring intellectual pulpit lecturers. And why church social groups are doing well, with whom church members can have coffee at the church, chat online, or be amused at one another's trivial Facebook postings.

But trendy church offerings are nothing but replications of what the secular world already offers—without long-term financial commitment, lifelong regular attendance, and delusions of the afterlife. The world offers music of all sorts, from inspirational, hip hop, country, rock, jazz, blues, and even environmental music, like that of John Denver and Neil Young. There are also alternative uplifting Hollywood movies, relaxing concerts, funny theatrical and comedy shows, motivational talks, circuses, magic shows, Disney World, Universal Studio, family resorts, sports arenas, spas, and public beaches and parks, among numerous other venues where people can let off steam, enjoy family togetherness, and rejuvenate themselves.

Second.

Dogmatism. A growing number of churchgoers who have access to information are becoming more open-minded, especially among the new generation of well-educated professionals, as well as the youth. The world we now live in, values open-mindedness and critical thinking more than blind acceptance of a belief system. Many Christians now, more than ever, believe in gender equality, have the drive to explore new ideas and perspectives in life, have a more scientific outlook on human life and existence, and abhor clergies and institutions imposing on them what to believe.

Further, many Christians are also beginning to realize that their respective denominations do not hold exclusive rights to God and Heaven. There is now more openness to relate to one another, and to regard God and the paradise in the afterlife as universal rather than sectarian products.

Furthermore, the new generation of churchgoers is trending toward life empowerment rather than ideological indoctrination. Life-oriented teachings rather than theological theories are what attract them. Plus, the global community we're living in, abhors authoritarianism in any form. More and more Christians now want to see their church as a life-coach, a spiritual buddy, and social group, rather than an ideologue, a spiritual judge, or a celestial transporter.

Third.

Frustration resulting from a realization that the church is no more divine than any other worldly institution. Inside the church we also find lust for luxury and sex, financial fraud, gender and ethnic discriminations, maltreatment of others (such as bullying), elitism, politicking, and even cruelties. The sins of the church are many. The traditional approach of hiding the sins of the church, such as, "Don't look at the people, just look up to Jesus," "The church is not perfect," or worse, "The church as God-ordained is never wrong," don't work anymore.

Christians have learned to use their common sense more than their predecessors. A growing number of believers are awakening to the fact that the church is, in essence, nothing but a mundane human institution. An institution that has used people's sense of uncertainty to exploit and manipulate their consciences for hundreds of years now. An institution propagating ancient myths that have really nothing to do with the advancement of human life, and which, in fact, in many cases even degrades humanity.

Fourth.

Conflicts. Inside the church, conflicts are inevitable. Oftentimes the conflicts arise from the clash between conservative and liberal members. Conservatives stick to traditional church cultures, liberals wish to adopt a more contemporary cultural ambience. The conservatives regard themselves as more faithful to the truth than the liberals, who are bringing worldly influence to the church. The liberals regard themselves as open-minded and bringing more life to a dying church, while the conservative are clinging on to death.

The common clash is the style of music shaping the style of church services. Some churches think using drums and guitars is devilish. The conservatives think that lullaby-like classical music is holy, they regard contemporary music that stimulates body movements as wicked. Liberals enjoy sacred discotheques, and want to attract more people to God through their lively music. Conservatives want to be closer to God through subdued music. Both are nonsense.

The style of music and church service also brings with it the style of preaching. Those with lively music have a screaming type of preaching, with humor and laughter, and even shedding of tears and trances. Some pastors even call for aerobic dances at the altars. Conservative Christians abhor this as devilish, and would condemn churches doing this to be cast into the lake of fire.

Aside from ritual-rooted conflicts, personal conflicts also abound. Let's accept the fact that though the church claims that believers are born again, they condemn one another to burn in Hell also. This shows that, really, the so-called new birth is a false assumption. Inside a number of churches, animosity arises for not being elected to church leadership positions (regarded by many as a symbol of in-church social prestige), or for not being able to convince fellow church members that one's opinion of the Bible is true. So are more serious matters like bullying of the clergy by church members (or vice versa), politicking of leadership positions in the bureaucracy, and ethnic segregation.

The holy churches of Christianity are loaded with conflicts, more than any secular institution. But why can't the church of holy followers, worshiping a holy God, be holier than a conflict-ridden institution? From the Vatican to a local parish, from the Christian university to seminaries, the concept of the new birth has not proven itself viable in transforming human nature.

Fifth.

The inability of the church to meet the needs of its members. A lot of churches, particularly those belonging to established denominations like the Catholic, Anglican, Reformed, United Church, and Baptists, among others, are out of touch with the daily life struggles of their members. Most sermons, with the exception of sermons in more contemporary churches, are still about high-sounding theological theories rather than down-to-Earth empowering talks.

Of course, you can't blame these clergies for doing so, that's what they got in their seminaries. Oftentimes you hear no difference between a boring philosophical lecture and a boring sermon, except for its lullaby-like qualities, luring listeners to sleep, or worse, into restless boredom. Every time members attend church, clergies bombard, or lambaste, them with theories of the afterlife and notions of the celestial. Forgetting that their adherents are earthly human beings living in the present real world, confronted with real challenges of life—broken marriages and families, drug and alcohol addictions, financial difficulties (struggling to make ends meet while being annoyed by tithes, offerings, and church donations), sickness and death, among the many trials of human life.

Think it through.

I don't mean that the church will solve all the problems of this world. No one can do that. God, almighty and all-knowing, should have resolved that at the outset. The reality is that no god or goddess of any religion can do that. But for the church to be so obsessed with making people pledge allegiance to its religious ideology, while ignoring the difficulties of their everyday life, is both a lunacy and a heartless exploitation.

Secular counselors can do a better job in empowering people to cope with life. That's why, in the tough world of the military, chaplaincy should be replaced with professional counseling. So too in hospitals, seniors' homes, and rehabilitation centers, among others. It's a huge waste of money employing chaplains who do nothing but market ancient tales of the afterlife, when professional counselors and motivational speakers can more effectively inspire courage, optimism, and transformation in the lives of people in need.

The world needs an alternative synthesis to religion in general, and the church in particular, a synthesis that enhances our humanity without controlling our everyday life and our perception of human destiny.

23
How Believers Become Atheists

It all starts from a frustrating experience in the church, then one frustration leads to another. The frustration may have started from a conflict with a church member, finding the pastor's sermon irrelevant, disagreement with how the church is run, a clash of opinion on doctrinal matters, or even a conflict with the pastor. Left unresolved, the frustration builds up until the believer decides to leave the church.

Upon leaving the church, believers either explore other Christian churches or remain believers of God without attending church, becoming spiritual but not religious; or begin to entertain other religious views, and even secular concepts. When believers explore other denominations, they have begun a journey of openness. It means the once-sectarian followers are now open to wider Christian traditions.

But with that openness, spiritual restlessness also sets in. Believers are now seeking for something more profound than mere sectarian faith, something universal, yet more fulfilling, which meaningfully addresses the crucial issues of human life and existence. They also become more rational rather than being a religious gullible. They begin to use reason and common sense in taking a closer look at Christian faith in its various forms, and sensibly seek for alternatives.

If the now journeying believers are lucky to find a caring and more sensible fellowship, they might stay. But though those who have already developed a critical disposition of faith may stay for a while, they eventually just sneak out. Others might also be curious of what religions other than Christianity, or hybrid approaches to spirituality, may offer. If they remain interested in spirituality, they may profess to be spiritual but not religious. That simply means they now abhor institutionalized religion, like the church.

That evolution may continue. Believers without regular indoctrination may develop an inclination to a secular outlook in life. This inclination, when coupled with crisis situations, would enable them to take a second look at religious claims, like the God who cares and answers prayers, the sacredness of the Bible, and the facts of the promised paradise in the hereafter. This now is the crossroad of one's awakening to the reality of religion. Then the question, "Does God really exist?" becomes the bottom line.

When faithful believers look at nature and all that happens in the world, they look at it from the perspective of religion. The unexplainable is always explained as mystery belonging to God. When believers are in an awakening stage, evolving from being myth-driven to reason-driven, they become open to scientific and logical explanations. Then they see themselves no longer preoccupied by religious traditions and doctrines, but by what makes real sense in life.

After realizing that religion and God are mere myths, they are then becoming ex-believers, slowly releasing themselves from the religiously-conditioned conscience that hooked them. At times, a foreboding may confront them, and they find themselves wrestling with common sense to transcend superstitious mystical feelings. They may keep it to themselves, having no secular, or atheist friends, to confide with yet. That loneliness may lead them to a relapse to religion, especially when they meet evangelistic-minded former religious friends, or people from other churches determined to win them back to the fold.

Now comes the challenge of their lives. If believers finally become atheists, how can they cope with the challenges of life? That's where secular people need to work and prove that, indeed, acts of random kindness, and the heart for humanity, are not only religious claims but common universal values that can be realized even more meaningfully without the exploitation of institutionalized myths.

Presently, atheism is becoming a movement. As a movement, it needs to focus not just on promoting its concepts but also on how it can empower fellow humans in living better lives. Otherwise, the movement to liberate our society from the shackles of religious myth simply becomes another ideology, just an anti-mindedness against religion, or a philosophy irrelevant to everyday human life. The Sunday Assembly and the social networks (even online dating) of atheists and other seculars, as well as the School of

Life, are a good beginning. But it needs to blossom.

Our society direly needs an empowering alternative to religion so we may enhance our profound sensibilities to the meanings and implications of our human existence and everyday lives. It's good to know, though, that the trend started by Silicon Valley to vivify the workplace environment is bringing fresh meaning to everyday workplace life in terms of nurturing human connections and releasing the pressures of daily life while stirring creativity and productivity that, in a way, church cannot offer. Now we know the possibilities for finding alternatives to empower, to cope with, and enjoy, our divine life is possible, and bountiful, given our inventiveness.

So why are believers becoming atheists?

Because they have already realized that religion and God are nothing but myths recycled from ancient cultures revised and then institutionalized into a church complete with organizational structures, products and services. And they begin to see better alternatives.

24
Church Transformation Needed

The churches of Christianity need to be born again! "Nonsense!" the conservative Christians would scream. "Are you kidding me?" the liberal Christians might say. "I don't care," the secular would most likely respond. "Hmm," an enterprising pastor wanting to make a stunt might react. But well, whatever your reaction might be, let me, an atheist still hiding under a Christian garb, just share my thoughts on what transformation the church needs.

One.

Change of genre from fiction to non-fiction, particularly the how-to kind. Loaded with myths of the ancient of times, for hundreds of years, having enjoyed the luxuries that came alongside people's ardor for fantasy, the church now needs to change its genre to something more earthly.

Yes, people are curious about aliens and everything extraterrestrial, but not the kind of fantasy that religion offers any-more. Many kids nowadays are still thrilled with Star Wars, but Bible stories for many are not fun anymore. Few kids now are thrilled by a slingshot. Lightsabers, or a spider's web are more interesting to them.

Stop the dumb religious theatrics and begin to help shape a better world to live in. Don't be so celestial that you forget humans are still earthly. Guide people how to live a better life, how to deal with the trials of life, what to do when marriages and families are broken. Don't just scream, "Get the devil out of here!" While marriage and the families are breaking down.

And can you also share some of your hidden wealth and resources to help people become entrepreneurs, rather than perpetual beggars? Remember Jesus said it's hard for rich people to enter Heaven? Another thing, yes, fiction is entertaining, but, well, you still can't beat Hollywood, so please help us experience meaning in our life in "the now." Reserve the fictional paradise in the hereafter for yourselves.

Second.

Get active! For hundreds of years you have lived a mostly sedentary life. Two thousand years of living a sedentary life is a really long time. See how fat your belly has become? See the tons of foods you have consumed. It could have fed a crowd of hungry people, much more in fact than the five thousand Jesus fed.

You need to change your lifestyle from a sedentary indoor life to an active outdoor one. Go to the marketplaces and the slums. Meet people where they are. Talk to them, listen, and identify with their daily struggles. Go with them, and help them make it through the ragged edges of life. It will make you healthier and more relevant.

And another thing, especially for your theologians, living in ivory towers preoccupied with playing with ideological hobby horses, imagining theories expressed in high-sounding words, doesn't make sense anymore! Ask most people on the street and they will tell you the same. Stop philosophizing, please, while the rest of us are trying to make ends meet, and just want to enjoy life—I mean real life, that the gods and goddesses of Olympus would envy.

Third.

Be a hugger. Stop that silly game of "loves me, loves me not." The world now appreciates inclusion rather than exclusion, acceptance rather than rejection. I know you feel you can't live without excluding others, because from the beginning when you became a church, you couldn't help but exclude others. And so you made your own sectarian dogma and rituals to preserve your exclusive existence while you fought with one another as competitors for Heaven.

But the time has now come for you to transcend your sectarianism and just be open to one another as belonging to one universal family of the God you worship. After all, you believe that Jesus is universal, as is the Heaven he offers. Then, when you learn to embrace one another, regardless of your petty sectarian theories (that are both fanciful and silly), don't also forget to embrace other divine human beings who have been relegated to the fringes by your aloof, if not arrogant, predecessors. You know there are a lot of human beings longing for their lives to be recognized as divine also.

By the way, the word of God says that all human beings came from one sacred root, so, in a sense, if you really believe in God's word, you should also regard all humans as equally sacred and dignified. I believe human life is sacred (one of the few things I'm religious about), regardless of gender, ethnicity, economic status, ideology (political or religious), and geographical origin.

If you just hug the rich, people will think you're just after their money. Sorry, I know that's your secret. If you hug men only, people will think you're chauvinist, if not a woman-hater. Don't hate women. Holy men could never be born without lovely women. Besides, Jesus even compared the church to a gorgeous bride. I bet Jesus must have loved women too. So don't be embarrassed of loving women and according them due respect and equal recognition. So are people whose gender you traditionally condemned to Hell. If you only hug those people inside your enclave, people will think you're a bigot. So I hope you'll hug everyone, so sweet and so warm, for we are all equally noble human beings.

Fourth.

Please stop whining about Earth while promoting the yet undiscovered extraterrestrial abode. When NASA discovers Heaven and Chris Hadfield broadcasts it, then we can talk about it with oozing enthusiasm. But for now let's talk about Earth. And please avoid scaring people to Hell now.

There's still a lot of things to do so we could have a taste of Heaven on Earth. Let's enjoy life instead of being obsessed with condemning people to Hell, and get engaged in making life more beautiful and wonderful. Yes, there are really bad guys doing bad things, but let society handle that. We already have institutions that can do that. So why don't you take a more positive approach to human life by helping make life on Earth more heavenly.

Another very important issue. Remember the Garden of Eden? It was really a beautiful place to live, I imagine, although I really don't know much about it. Now, the Edenic places in this world are fast disappearing. Please don't pray just for the extraterrestrial Heaven, please help bring back the Garden of Eden to Earth. You taught that because of sin, God took the Garden out from Earth. Now let a righteous way of life restore the Garden. To be candid, don't just sit there on the mystical throne. Wake up, fight for justice to nature, and our universal right to live in the Garden of Eden.

Fifth.

Evolve from hunting and gathering to raising and catering. Most of your life you've only hunted and gathered. I know it's fun, but the world has evolved since you were first institutionalized. Way back in 325 CE, when you hunted and gathered, people thought it was cool. But not anymore! Anyway, you have already hunted and gathered yourself to obesity. Share!

Instead of hunting and gathering, begin raising a fresh civilization of caring and kindhearted people. Shed your excess fat. And make use of it to fuel your acts of random kindness. Not the calculated ones intended to gather ideological converts, but those which help shape a more optimistic life. Instead of preparing for a banquet in your imaginary heavenly kingdom, feed the hungry in our real present world.

Use your resources to cater to our varied needs in life: emotionally, intellectually, socially, and also economically. That is if you can spare some of your extra fat for constructive use. Instead of saving people from the horrors of the forthcoming Hell, it would be more human to be saving people from the horrors of injustice and wanton human abuses. Help the poor and suffering people taste, or better still, live, in Heaven while still living on Earth. That's more truly divine than mere sermonizing.

And one more matter. Be more like a feature writer than a paparazzi. In my view, the feature writer enhances our understanding and appreciation of the beauty and wonders of nature and human life, while the paparazzi simply want to sell embarrassing moments in one's life. For one, it's all about writing. For the other, it's all about selling. One is more about culture and the art of living. The other is more about selling the anomalies of life. Making money by brainwashing people into believing they are sinners, and then selling them a one way ticket to Heaven (to avoid Hell) is even more exploitive than intruding into one's privacy to have money to buy bread.

The divinity of the church does not lie in its being elevated to royalty and pomp, but in its altruistic descent to the slums. Godliness is not something mystical, it's practical. The church that's preoccupied with preaching is merely a religious ideologue. The church that's focused on serving the deprived is the healer of humanity.

25
Comparative Myths: Christian and Others

Myths play a role in the catharsis of our soul. They entertain us, stir our imaginations, and motivate us to go beyond, because they embody the fusion of our aspirations and frustrations in life. And as the fusion of the good and the bad, they either help shape the progress of our human civilization, or degrade it. Myths pervade our world literatures from the ancient to the present. In fact, Hollywood thrives on myths. And we love them.

The difference between other myths and religion, though, is that in religion we have myths that are institutionalized, imposed upon others, and used to control people's lives. Imagine if DC Comics organized a social institution for the worship of Superman, and Marvel Comics the worship of Thor. Every week, each (I'm not sure which one is more Catholic or more Protestant than the other) of the competing "churches" would sing praises to their respective hero and propagate him as the only savior of the world, one being a modern embodiment of a superhuman being, the other a carry-over of an ancient myth. Both are extraterrestrial super-beings who became human, experienced temporary death, and were resurrected to become even more motivated extraterrestrial saviors of humanity.

Those who become members of the worship club would be required to live according to what Time Warner and Walt Disney would prescribe. Worshippers would pay tithes and offerings for attending services, and be faithful to the teachings of the superheroes. Otherwise, when the world ended (as being devastated by global warming or devastated by aliens), they'd lose the opportunity to be in paradise (would a Mars settlement work?) and suffer Hell on Earth. Worshippers would become so dedicated that they were even willing to die for the notion of worshipping their superhero.

Silly, outrageous, and insane? Let's take a look at the sample of what the churches believe and propagate, and see if they make sense and are worth dying for.

The Catholic.

Originated the notion that: A) Jesus is God (after many others who contended that Jesus was just human were either driven away, or tortured), and B) Outside the Catholic Church there's no salvation.

The Orthodox.

The Orthodox (whether it's Eastern or Oriental), there's no place for the pope in the church. The Holy Spirit came out of the body of Jesus, as opposed to the Catholic belief that it came from both Jesus and the Father. Both are really paranormal anyways.

The Lutherans.

With its squabbling sub-brands, affirmation is what it takes to go to Heaven (so going to Heaven is brainwave-activated, cooler than voice-activated).

The Anglican.

Invented the King James Bible (ensuring it's not a Catholic one) to cater to Anglican doctrines.

The Reformed.

With its mega-variants, are serious about humans having no choice to be, or not to be, in paradise.

The Baptists.

With sickening myriads of competing brands, Baptists believe that water is the portal to paradise (I wish they'd launch a crusade against water pollution).

The Assembly of God.

With its dizzying numbers of rival Pentecostals. No trance mumbling, no assurance of Heaven.

The Seventh-day Adventists.

If you go to church on Sunday you'll have the mark of the devil. God hates Sunday.

The Jehovah's Witnesses.

Jesus is not God, he is a mere human, but if you're dying and need blood, avoid blood transfusion if you don't want to miss paradise. Die miserably.

The Mormons.

Human beings can be gods and goddesses (of what?) too, but only through the Mormon Temple. By the way, God made a mistake about polygamy.

The Christian Science.

Sick and poor, healthy and rich? No difference! Everything is just an illusion (consequentially, including Mary Baker Eddy and her church).

Want to die for any of these sillinesses? It's up to you. Just wake to common sense. Furthermore, compare these ancient myths with Christian ones:

Creation of the universe.

Chaos, a Greek primordial god characterized as the void state from which all things came from, created Gaia (the Earth) and Uranus (the Sky) upon separating them. Out of Chaos also came Tartaros (the Underworld), Nyx (the Night), and Erebos (the Darkness of the Underworld).

Genesis (1: 1-5, NIV) said:

> In the beginning God (Chaos?) Created the heavens (Uranus?) and the Earth (Gaia?). Now the

> earth was formless and empty (Chaos?), darkness (Erebos?) was over the surface of the deep (Tartarus?)... The darkness he called "night" (Nyx?).

Take note, the ancient Greek myth, although written by Hesiod circa 700 BC, existed much earlier as a long cherished story of how the world began.

Genesis (1: 6-8 NLT) also said:

> Then God said, "Let there be a space between the waters, to separate the waters of the Heavens from the waters of the earth ... God made this space to separate the waters of the earth from the waters of the Heavens. God called the space "sky."

The notion of the primordial God separating the Earth from Heaven was an established myth the Babylonians had been telling long before Genesis was written. In the *Enuma Elish,* Marduk (the primordial God) created Heaven and Earth out of Tiamat (primeval waters).

Do modern humans still believe that the heavens, or the sky and Earth, were created by a primordial god separating the two realms out of an ocean? Don't be so dumb. *First*, our sky is not the only atmosphere. *Second*, our ground is not the only ground, nor our planet the only planet.

Flood myths.

The world, full of bodies of water, with tides rising and flooding seashores, and rains that, oftentimes, destroy farmlands, since the ancient times (especially in an ancient agricultural societies) has been filled with all sorts of flood myths. These myths abound from the ancient Middle East (like the Sumerian Flood), to Africa, to Asia-Pacific (like China's Miao Flood Myth), Europe, and the Americas (like the Inca's Unu Pachakuti myth).[27] Fundamentalist theologians (ironically, including so-called Christian scientists), contend that the pervasiveness of flood myths indicate that the story of Noah is true.

First, most of the ancient flood myths are more ancient than the story of Noah. *Second*, most ancient civilizations did not know who Noah and his family were. The only viable explanation is that the writer of Genesis simply copied the myth and adapted it to the ancient Jewish emerging culture. Jewish scholars will testify that the Old Testament (which, really, is their ancient literature, not

Christian's) is about spirituality, not actual history.

Dying and resurrecting God.

The myth of dying and resurrecting God is also common among the ancients. So common that many modern scholars (like Martin Hengel, Barry Powell, and Peter Wick) pointed out significant similarities between the Greek God Dionysius and Jesus. Consequently, they also pointed out similarities between Dionysian and Christian religions.

Deities also related to the Christian belief of a dying God are the Roman god Mithras, and the Egyptian Horus (scholars like Tom Gerald Massey and Tom Harpur pointed this out), among others, whose tales are all more ancient than the story of Jesus as the God who died and resurrected. So the belief that Jesus was the incarnate God who died, then resurrected, was simply borrowed from other ancient beliefs.

There are numerous other elements of religion which arise from myth: angels, the battle of the gods (like between God and Satan), gods and goddess who offered their lives to save humanity, to divine scriptures (all religions claim their scriptures are God-given), and Heaven and Hell. Though the characters and settings may be different, (simply because they are all adapted to a particular geography and culture), the essence is still the same (even of the modern Hollywood super hero myths)—meant to entertain our soul while giving expression to our deepest wishes to control the bad forces of the universe, and come out of tragedies victorious.

It's one thing to enjoy Santa Claus. It's another thing to use Santa Claus to regulate our lives, direct the advancement of our civilization, and determine our universal destiny.

Why Secularism?

26
The Psyche of Believers

Years back, I couldn't understand why atheists didn't believe in God because, for me, the universe was full of proof that God existed. Now I can't understand why theists believe in God, because there's nothing in the universe that proves that God exists.

Had I realized the true nature of religion much earlier, I would have not left my childhood dream to design machines and invent life-enhancing gadgets to make a lot of money. Or I could have gone to medical school and fulfilled my dad's wish. My dad couldn't afford it, but a relative promised to help. Although my dad was religious, particularly during Holy Week, he was also a practical man.

But why was I so dogged a believer of religion? For quite a number of years, no one could sway me to forsake my faith. Why didn't I process information that could have otherwise liberated me from the fetters of religious myth earlier? The answer is simple, yet baffling. Early in life, I quickly developed a pious mentality. And how did the pious mentality work?

One.

It's a calculated learning. Did I also wish to learn other views, like doctrines of other denominations or even atheism? Yes! But every time I read and learned other views, I always sought to convince myself of the non-veracity of other views, and learned how to argue against them, defending my sectarian view as the only truth.

I refused to sincerely know what other people thought, because my assumption was always that other views are false. I always believed that I, and my fellow believers, held the only secret, the only knowledge-code, to Heaven and God. Although I recognized that we were just a handful compared to the billions of world population, we believed that out of the many we were the chosen few. It's that same delusion of being chosen by God among the many that perpetuates religious madness.

But damn it, it's only now that I realize that reality is much wider than my petty notions.

Two.

Denial syndrome. I and my fellow believers refused to entertain the possibility that our sectarian beliefs were flawed, and false. There could be no other truth for me aside from my denominational interpretation of the Bible. More so, there could be no truth to secular views, especially atheism, agnosticism, or humanism, because for me it was clear that there was, and ever would be, God. And there was no other God aside from my denominational Christian God. Even if, at times, I was confused by the interchange of God and Jesus when praying.

My stance was always to deny the truthfulness of other views, religious and secular alike. I was so dumb, though, not to realize, despite knowing it, that my beliefs were human-made. Formulated first by wannabe oracles, then by professional oracles (theologians), who also read other people's books and views, and thus formulated our sectarian doctrinal statements. It baffles me now how theologians also end up believing their theological assumptions are the only God-given truths.

Silly me, I never realized that the guys who formulated our beliefs were just squabbling for the mundane votes in the deification of their respective notions. It didn't matter whether their notions were ridiculous, or puzzling, as long as they were voted sacred, church members will just end up saying amen to it.

Three.

Disoriented commitment. My commitment was ever with my denomination. I was zealous about a lifetime career of expanding my church membership because it meant gathering people for Heaven. I was dogged in defending my church's beliefs because it was the only truth that could bring salvation to humanity. In my delusion, I became not just a clergyman, but a theologian-clergyman.

I committed myself to preserving and advancing our church beliefs. With pride, I affirmed that there was no other career on Earth more noble than saving the souls of people. My commitment to my beliefs, my church, and my holy career, blinded me. My illusory world hypnotically disabled my common sense.

Ahhh! I'm screaming to the top of my voice now! Realizing the madness that wasted my life.

Four.

Confused equation. I equated my beliefs and my church as directly God-ordained, and the universe as absolutely created by God according to Genesis (which isn't even Christian, but Jewish that denies the deification of Jesus).

I knew the Old Testament was Jewish, but I assumed the Old Testament was written for Christians and speaking only of Christian faith, not knowing that Judaism is a totally different religion. I knew that Jews did not believe in Jesus, but my assumption, as is assumed by most Christians, was that

Jesus came to correct the mistakes of the ancient Jews. While knowing that the Jews rejected Jesus as the messiah, I still assumed they worshipped the same Christian God. I even thought that being the messiah was the same as being God, not knowing that being the messiah meant being the rebel leader.

I also presumed that my church had existed since the beginning of time. Ignoring the fact that long after human civilization had already begun, when followers of Jesus, coming from varied cultural and philosophical backgrounds, were squabbling and fighting for dominance—it was only then that the Christian church was organized. Not in Heaven but on Earth. Organized, not because of goodwill, but because of ill will.

I dumbly assumed that Moses wrote an actual account of the creation of the universe, when he wasn't even an atom on Earth. Humanity had not even emerged. Dumb! Humanity wasn't even a sperm when the universe began. Now I see more probability in an ancient astronaut theory than the Genesis creation story. And why would God tell the origin of the world just in Hebrew? Why not in Chinese, Sumerian, or Indo-Aryan, that are much earlier? The truth is, Jewish scholars regard the Torah, or the Old Testament, as a spiritual book rather than a factual narrative.

Robert Harris, an Associate Professor at the Jewish Theological Seminary, affirms this long-held view. Reacting to an article posted in *Huffington Post* on February 6, 2014 about the discovery by researchers from Tel Aviv University of a major discrepancy in Biblical history, he wrote:

While these findings may have been published recently, those of us on the inside have known the essential facts for a generation now.... This is just one of many anachronisms in the Bible, but these do not detract from its sanctity, because it is a spiritual source, not a historical one.[28]

William Dever, a noted retired Professor of Near Eastern Archaeology and Anthropology at the University of Arizona in Tucson, added:

We want to make the Bible history. Many people think it has to be history or nothing. But there is no word for history in the Hebrew Bible. In other words, what did the biblical writers think they were doing? Writing objective history? No. That's a modern discipline. They were telling stories. They wanted you to know what these purported events mean.[29]

I trembled at the thought of entertaining

even just a bit of doubt on the truthfulness of my church beliefs. Equating theoretical criticism as an act of losing my soul to the Devil, forfeiting Heaven, and becoming an enemy of God. I was ideologically deluded and enslaved. I was deceived and entrapped by the church, even if it was composed of seemingly good-hearted people, who like me were also ideologically enslaved by the delusions of their own making.

To err is human, to continue in error is divinely stupid.

Fifth.

Just plain stupidity. I believed that all knowledge and science should always be geared, not just toward the Bible, but particularly to my own church's doctrines. It's the kind of stupidity I inherited from my ancient Christian predecessors in the Medieval era, who regulated science, and even geographical explorations, in accordance with the Church's fanciful ideas.

So, as a young and educated professional, I would allow a bit of the idea of evolution, because I, and the church, could not deny it anymore. Not Darwin's theory, though, but a micro-evolution theory, that God created everything and then allowed sub-species to evolve, with all the major animal species we now have descending from Noah's Ark. I would relate the discoveries of surface movements around the world as proof of Noah's Flood. And would even regard photos of galaxy formations billions of light years away as portraying the face of God, proving his existence; although, I haven't really seen a Facebook of Jesus, more so God. I just assumed the portrayal of Jesus and God as long-haired and bearded Europeans by Medieval artists were real.

I would always affirm people's personal experiences of being saved from desperate situations as just one of the many examples of God's miracles. Meanwhile I took for granted the lack of God's saving miracles amid countless global tragedies and miseries. Ironically, in my stupidity, I would still affirm that he was there, lovingly watching and caring for humanity. I just couldn't see reality with my common sense. I would even easily accept claims of people seeing Heaven and Jesus as real without considering that people dream all sorts of things every night, and will hallucinate in critical physical-mental states.

I called myself a faithful Christian, a loving person who loved his neighbors as Jesus did. But I hated atheists, agnostics, humanists, and people belonging to other denominations and religions. Because they just couldn't get it. They couldn't see the absolute validity of my church's beliefs. Anyway, I said to myself, "I'll just leave it up to God to burn them in Hell."

Think it through.

Religion is so divine for many believers that they are willing to be dehumanized by it. Building a whole system of life out of the varied ideas of an illusory God and Heaven is one of the greatest embarrassments in our intellectual development as *Homo sapiens sapiens*. That's our species with two "wisdoms." Probably we need another one to make us realize the folly of religion. Only by breaking free from the world of myth can we appreciate the grandeur of human life and existence.

27
Why We Need Alternative Secular Values

Why do we need alternative sensible secular values? Because church values are based on myths, financially and psychologically exploitive, and societally controlling.

But can there be values outside religion? The religious would instantly say, "No!" Because for them, values, morality and right sense of living only come from God. And they don't mean gods of other religions, they mean their respective particular God.

So, really, what the religious call a value system is nothing but a sectarian ideology that they intend to impose on the rest of the world. The imposition might be passive, doggedly propagating it and letting people decide on its merits. Or active, imposed in religious countries, like those of the Middle East. In essence, religion is culturally imperialistic.

So why do we need alternative and sensible secular values?

First.

So we can be free from the fetters of institutionalized religious myths. Religion has conditioned the minds of countless divine human beings, for myriads of generations. Today, we no longer think the Earth is the center of the universe. Nor that universal existence originated from Earth. But what about universal existence as a primeval creation of an ancient deity adopted by the writer of Genesis, from among the wide array of ancient Middle Eastern gods and goddesses?

Civilized modern humans nurture and cherish freedom, physically, socially, emotionally, and intellectually. Religion has enslaved us, in many aspects of our lives; it has deceived us into committing ourselves to attending weekly church services due to the fear of Hell and the wish for Heaven. Through such fear and desire, it has also emotionally exploited us. By making us believe that humanity's future is exclusive to our respective religious organization, religion has stunted our ability for analytical-critically thinking.

With such stunted thinking, we end up committing our time and hard-earned money to promoting the dominion of our respective religious ideology. Our feet have been tied, our mouths zipped, our eyes blinded, our ears stuffed, our hands conditioned to open to church coffers. Our minds have been clouded by mythical fantasies. We need to be free from mythical constraints so we can enjoy progressive human lives.

It's time for us to untie our feet and walk to freedom. Unzip our mouths and speak the truth about religious myths and ideologies. Open our eyes and begin to see the wider world. Unclog our ears so we may hear more life-empowering words. Recondition our hands to support more practical and beneficial causes. And clear our minds so that we can finally realize that there's a world wider, more beautiful, and more meaningful, than any religious enclave.

Second.

So we can develop more inclusive values. No need to argue, just slowly open our minds, while letting go of our preconceived beliefs, with honest hearts, and see the real nature of religion.

Candidly, religion is exclusivist. For it's in exclusion that religion thrives. Each religion, each church, thrives first by claiming to have a unique message, or divine knowledge, not found in others; then, by doggedly imposing such claim. In the past, religion did it by grand invasion. Now it's done by glamorous marketing, and afterwards by controlling people's consciences, locking them into exclusive long-term commitments (that makes long-term cell phone commitment look very trivial).

At times, we see religious groups (including their dummies), protesting against what they tag as suppression of religious freedom and inclusion. But the truth is, behind the masquerade we see the leading institutions for suppressing freedom and inclusion. Religion suppresses freedom in tricky ways—innocent like a dove, predatory like a serpent.

When a religious group protests against a social issue, it's because it thinks of itself as the absolute authority of morals and values. Religious organizations deeply believe that its own values should govern the rest of the society, and even the world. Everything outside its own belief system is devilish and anti-God. Take note, too, that there's not only one religion, but a dizzying myriad of them, each claiming to be *the* exclusive repository of morals and values that should govern humanity.

The leading universities of the world, instead of perpetuating theology departments, should begin trending toward developing sensible and inclusive secular values as an alternative to religious belief systems. We need values that are inclusive and which promote wider acceptance of our fellow human beings, regardless of the superficial labels we discriminately impose. Our very humanity doesn't inhere in our superficial social statuses. On the contrary, the superficial social statues we invented and imposed on others threaten our very humanity.

Religion treats those who don't share their exclusive belief system as enemies. That stirs them to wage the war of God against their fellow humans. That's ridiculous! Because if God were real and omnipotent, why couldn't he wage war himself, and in a split second declare victory? Others who are not members of the same religious club are regarded as doomed to Hell, so they either need to be thrown out of society or converted into one's club. I could go on and on citing issues of religious exclusivism and imperialism, but the bottom line is—for our society to be free and inclusive we need to be free from the domination of religion.

Religion, by virtue of its religious ideology, has become an expert of excluding people. What we need for the recognition of essential human equality is the development of more inclusive and humanizing secular values.

Third.

So our souls will not be commercialized. Religion has done nothing constructive beyond its religiously calculated humanitarian endeavors (albeit easing some human suffering).

Every humanitarian endeavor the church does is always done with the expectation that it will help propagate the church's belief system, and gain more converts. Converts then are expected to be supporters of the church—socially (in terms of regular and long-term church attendance and physical support to its services) and financially (in terms of regular and long-term faithfulness in giving tithes and offerings).

In the end, people find themselves trapped (for a long time, until they build the courage to get free) in the restrictive world of the church. Churchgoers then believe that it's only by socially and financially sustaining the church that they can sustain the well-being of their souls, and their future in the afterlife. Each church, including the independent churches that pop up like mushrooms feeding on the human soul, competes for soul-customers, if not for control of the soul market.

With only a theatrical charisma, an idea of the afterlife, and claim of God's calling, independent religious entrepreneurs, as well as established churches, can rake in millions of bucks, tax free. The maintenance and growth of their coffers are always ensured by the believer's conviction of investing in a guaranteed lifetime, and beyond, insurance. Of course, the church, like other social institutions, could not exist without monetary support. But for a social institution to bilk people of their money for the promise of a mythical paradise is, honestly speaking, a scam.

Lately, the Mars One project has enthused a number of people around the world. With careful scientific and technological considerations, we now know that it's possible to create a human settlement on Mars. But imagine, for example, American Airlines offering a one-way ticket for the idea of a possible paradise on Mars that would ensure perfect health and longevity. There's no scientific verification of the existence of the paradise yet, but AA executives believe it's there somewhere, and customers are required not just to pay a one-time fee, but to contribute ten percent of their monthly income, and also give regular weekly offerings, for life. Aside from that, they are also required to attend weekend workshops. I bet the Feds would quickly jump in and close the meeting place and handcuff the executives. The global mass media would buzz—the dumbest and silliest scam ever. But isn't that what religion is doing? Selling myths and commercializing the human soul?

What we need, instead of religion, is the development of sensible secular values that enhance our sense of humanity, empowering us to cope with the challenges of everyday life, and inspiring us in shaping a more equitable and dignified future.

Fourth.

So our consciences won't be exploited and controlled. Not only are our souls being commercialized by religion, but also our consciences are being exploited and controlled.

Because of our deep wish for certainty about the future (both near and beyond), religion offers us myths to ensure our wishes are nurtured. In the process of nurturing our fantasies, religion then exploits and controls our consciences by making us believe that it's only by remaining within its enclave, and faithfully supporting it for life, that we can we be assured of our future.

Thus, the church controls our consciences and makes us believe that it has a great say in our destiny. Instead of teaching us the art of daily living, the church becomes the overarching control of our lives. Instead of inspiring us to shape a better future, the church makes us fantasize about an illusory utopia. Instead of helping us cope with the realities of human life, it instills in us the spirit of escapism (by doggedly offering us a getaway to the mystical world through an imaginary extraterrestrial super-being).

Conscience is not independent from our mental processes, as if it were a separate voice God uses to communicate to us. It's a form of mental reaction-feeling we develop through years of indoctrination. In the many aspects of our lives, we develop a lot of conditioned-thinking, and conscience is no different from that. For some, seeing spicy foods makes them salivate; for others it makes them lose appetite. For the poor and the homeless, living in a modest subsidized housing is a luxury; for the wealthy it's a misery.

For most of us, seeing gorgeous ladies on the beach wearing swimsuits is a pleasure; for others it's a mortal sin (ironically, not sinful for those watching but for those wearing it). For the Catholics, missing Communion for months would cause a bothered conscience, while other Christians wouldn't care. For Muslims and the Adventists, eating pork is a sin, while for the Jehovah's Witness blood transfusion is.

So in all these, who speaks to us? No supernatural being called God. It's simply what we are used to thinking and regarding as pleasing or displeasing, normal or sinful, relative to the environment that shapes our thinking.

When someone (person or organization) controls our thinking-environment, that someone also controls our outlook in life. Once our outlook in life is controlled, we become easy prey for exploitation and further psychological control. There's nothing so liberating as having values free from the control of others, especially myths.

Yes, we need social control, a social thermostat that seeks the level of our common good. But not the kind of control that hooks us to a variety of conflicting myths, and imposes subjugation upon us, to the whims of self-claimed oracles of the mystical world. That's too much of a lunacy.

Fifth.

So we can have a more practical and life-empowering outlook on human life and universal existence. The churches of Christianity are preoccupied with propagating their varied and conflicting ideas about God and Heaven. It's all about the promotion of ideas that are not yet, and will never be, proven as facts, since they are all theories about imaginative beings and the world.

In essence, religions that focus on the worship of a particular God are no different from one another. Theistic religions are no different from what Western academia (heavily influenced by Christianity) calls ancient mythology, like the gods and goddess of the ancient Romans, the Greeks, Babylon, the Incas, ancient China, and Japan, among others. Theistic religions are all focused on worshipping a god, or gods, that were adopted from previous traditions and revised to suit a founder's notion and cultural context. Religion is all an imposition of mythological ideologies.

Yes, there are mega-churches where the teachings are more motivational than doctrinal. But those motivational-oriented preachers are worse than secular motivational speakers. Why?

First, secular motivational speakers (what I call SMS's) charge by the workshop, conference, or seminar. Motivational religious preachers (what I call MRP's) impose a lifetime of regular financial commitment.

Second, SMS's deals about practical matters, like workplace environment, leadership, coping with the stresses of life, using scientific studies (and, at times, clinical) and actual experiences. MRP's relate their suppositions about what the unseen God has said, and should say. Usually, the fans of SMS's become more enthused about life, while the fans of MRP's end up becoming dogged church members.

Third, SMS's empower people to manage and direct their lives so they (including their loved ones, families, and friends) can enjoy their present lives. MRP's tell people to fantasize a life in the afterlife. When it comes to film, usually I like fiction because it's very imaginative, but in the case of living my life, I would certainly love to approach it from a non-fictional perspective.

Think it through.

Values that are not concerned about the enhancement of our daily lives are nothing but mythical ideologies. For religious fanatics, there's no real world outside their respective fantasy-worlds, no moral human beings outside their ideological prison camps, no future for the human race outside their mysticism.

For civilized humanity, the real world is the world in which we now live. The real people are the people we meet every day. Our concretely viable hope for the future is the advancement of our human species toward a more dignified collective life. Religion cannot provide this, and even deforms it, because of its insistence on its exclusivist and widely conflicting mythical ideologies.

28
The Prospects of a New "Faith"

More and more people are leaving churches and they need alternative values. In 2012, CNN reported a significant 25% rise (equivalent to 1 in 5 Americans, or 33 million Americans) of non-religious Americans in a five-year survey period.[30] And 88% of the non-religious are not looking for religion. *Huff-*

ington Post also noted the rise of atheism in America[31], the bulwark of evangelical Christianity. This indicates that more and more believers are awakening to the fact that religion has no significance in their lives.

Theism is declining, particularly among the younger generations, who are more open-minded and eschew authoritarian thinking. Many once-faithful churchgoers now realize that the Heaven religion offers as the ultimate hope of humanity is a myth, as is the God the churches (and religion in general) impose upon the world to worship. Looking closely, we see no essential difference among the gods and goddesses religions offer—they are all imaginary superheroes their proponents wanted the world to worship.

Thus, we need a sensible secular alternative to the mythical religious faith system. We need an alternative anchor for our human soul (not the one that goes out of our body and travels somewhere, I mean our psyches). We need fresh faith—a religionless faith—that nurtures our everyday life, while freeing us from ideological and mythological controls and exploitation. We need a new outlook in life that enhances our creative engagement with one another and the universe we live in. But what would this "new faith" looks like? I propose the following characteristics.

One.

Inclusive. It should promote inclusion rather than exclusion. No more of those nasty attitudes: "Holier-than-thou;" "I hold the only truth and you don't;" "Our enclave is divine and yours is wicked;" "Men only;" "Gays and lesbians will go to Hell" (imagine a fundamentalist preacher pronouncing condemnation with a foaming mouth); "Go with your own kind" (as in, make your own ethnic church); "My God will save my group but annihilate others;" "Unless you believe in what I believe you'll be doomed to Hell;" "All people are equal but others are more divine" (what a dummy irony). Religion is one of the reasons why we have exclusivism resulting in gender, ethnic and cultural discriminations.

Two.

Utilitarian. We need a new faith that enhances our collective common good, not the kind of faith system that only sees Heaven for a particular group of adherents. But the faith that inculcates in us the passion to contribute to our common good so, as one humanity, we can enjoy life together while ensuring our common future.

Sound like communism? No, it's more like a collective utilitarian consciousness of life, values that naturally incline us to join together in making life more beautiful. As social human beings, we have this natural tendency. We have seen this in times of crisis. We can make it a normal habit.

Three.

Practical and empowering. A new faith that does not lead us to sit in the pews for hours imagining how righteous we have become. Fantasizing about when we'll be like Casper, floating in the air, playing an ancient harp amid the peaceful ambiance of Heaven. But a kind of faith that makes us passionate about a proactive productive life that's beneficial to us (personally), to our families, and society in general.

We cannot make all poor people rich, nor create a utopia. But we need a new faith that motivates us when we are down, lifts us up when we are in the mire, and gives us the courage to pursue happiness in life amid difficulties. A faith like that of the garage or basement entrepreneurs who became mega-successful. A faith like that of inventors who created things to enhance our lives. A faith like that of life-oriented thinkers who offered us new ideas to explore and advance our civilization. A faith like that of tired and weary climbers who made it to the summit of Everest. A faith like that of the physically-challenged athletes who made it to gold in the Paralympics.

Above all, a fresh faith that leads us to savor the joys of everyday life while empowering us to cope with our finitudes.

Four.

Non-ideological and un-institutionalized. Why can't we have values that are not part of an institutionalized ideology imposed on its adherents, and is intended to be imposed to the whole world? Can we not have sensible values outside an imperialistic and invasive belief system? Faithful Christians would like us to think that there can be no values outside the church (in particular) and religion (in general), as the only source of values are religious myths.

It's not religion that created humanity, it's humans who created religion. We know that religion had a beginning in human reflections. We, humans, invented religion, so we could find a way to express our wishes and imagination.

In essence, religion started as an imaginative literary pursuit. Religious pioneers wrote what they imagined to be the origin of the universe, and how superhuman beings with amplified human abilities transcending our finitude would react to the realities of the world. In writing their wild imaginations, they also included their personal concepts of right and wrong, integrating their personal prejudices, biases, and preconceived notions.

So why do we need to be forever hooked to religious thinking, when human thinking and creativity is not confined in religious prejudices and biases? Humanity is bigger than religious adherents. Human life is wider than religiosity. Our universe is more immense than the mythical world created by religion. Our body of knowledge, science and technology, are much larger and richer than all ancient religious literatures combined. Enough of doctrines! Enough of theories of the hereafter! Enough of a way of life that promotes bigotry of others outside one's church! And enough stupidity in claiming that the future of humanity hinges on the church and its ancient belief traditions!

What we need are values that enhance our sense of humanity, enriches our role in the ecosystem of life, and deepens our awareness of our place in our immense universe.

Fifth.

Realistic. Yes, it's good to discuss the ideals of life. But too much idealizing becomes a hallucination, and hallucination causes abnormal lifestyles. What we need are values that, while working out the ideals of human life, also applies to the realities of daily human living.

Every day we hear children crying whose families are breaking down; kids trembling while resorting to drugs amid uncertainty of where to go; people going to work like zombies losing meaning in life. And all the church does is convince people to affirm their theories of God and Heaven as the only truth so they can expect miracles in their lives. Nonsense! Yes, the church may feed some hungry people, but feed them so they praise the name of Jesus. Church, or religion, rooted values are myth-driven and calculated-goodness intended for make more proselytes. What we, modern humans, need are realistic values intended for the common good.

Think it through.

Long before the churches of Christianity were organized, our human species survived in an even harsher world than we have now. Because, innate in us, are values that enabled us to survive and advance in our individual and collective evolution. The values of courage, kindness, common good, and a sense of what's right and wrong, are inherent in our nature. They are not an artificial creation of the church, nor of any religion.

These innate values enabled us to direct our ways, enjoy our lives, and find meaning in the joys and challenges of life. They are not meant to make us a people of the castle in the sky. Human values are meant to nurture our fullest enjoyment of present life, while directing us to shape a better viable future.

The new faith I'm proposing is not a religion or an institutionalized value system. It is a fresh outlook in life that inspires the rekindling of a personal sense for a more creative and utilitarian life.

29
The Ten Principles

Reflecting on the essentials of human life in relation to how we treat one another, I put into words what I realized were the foundations of living a sensible secular life.

The Ten Principles
One
Revere the sanctity of human life.

Human life should take priority over material goods or the pursuit of ideological causes.

Two.

Don't make humans a commodity.

We are dignified beings. Treating our fellow human beings as commodities degrades the very humanity of our species.

Three.

Honor all people's humanity and creative potential regardless of status.

We are all equally noble human beings, and have equal, complementary potentials for contributing to the betterment of our lives, and the advancement of our civilization.

Four.

Take a break from the stresses of everyday life to rejuvenate yourself and your relationships.

Life is useless when you wear yourself down to broken pieces. You need to take a break to relish your health and to take pleasure in your relationships.

Five.

Take care of your family.

Nothing is more fundamentally meaningful to the survival of our human race than a happy family.

Six.

Nurture your marriage.

We can either take it for granted to our misery, or nurture it to our bliss.

Seven.

Find contentment in life.

Insatiability is the root of all evil, for there's no end in insatiability but restive discontentment resulting in inhuman exploitation. Find delight in the varied levels of life.

Eight.

Be constructive in all aspects of life.

A penchant for a constructive way of life is the key to bringing paradise on Earth.

Nine.

Have a propensity for the common good.

A well-developed natural inclination for the common good is the root of acts of random kindness that alleviate the sufferings of humanity.

Ten.

Enjoy life in the present while shaping a better future.

Heaven is real when we seek to enjoy our present life while directing a pleasant future.

See? I told you we can have more sensible values outside religion. Now we can begin a fresh journey.

Epilogue
En Route to a Fresh Outlook in Human Life

Opening our minds to the wider realities of life,

> We find ourselves free from the fetters of religious myths,
>
> > then we see that indeed the world is much larger than we used to think.

Now we're on a fresh journey in life.

At first, we feel awkward, adapting to the brighter world outside our earlier dark enclaves.

But then, like babies excited to take their first step, we find life more exciting when we finally learn to walk, then leap and run (and for others even to do gymnastics and stunts) to enjoy a life of freedom!

From this time onward, our life will no longer be governed by an authoritarian ideology of the mythical world, but directed by our profound consciousness of the preciousness of human life and our desire to enjoy life to the fullest ...

Endnotes

[1] http://www.forbes.com/sites/kellyphillipserb/2013/10/24/vatican-suspends-bishop-of-bling-over-40-million-home-renovation/
[2] http://www.economist.com/node/21560536
[3] http://news.nationalpost.com/2013/03/08/wealth-of-roman-catholic-church-impossible-to-calculate/
[4] http://www.economywatch.com/news/infographic-megachurches-megabusinesses.05-09.html
[5] http://www.dailymail.co.uk/news/article-2280403/Evangelist-Benny-Hinns-son-arrested-Brazil-beating-deaf-dumb-man-fathers-events.html
[6] http://www.theledger.com/article/20050716/NEWS/507160317?tc=ar
[7] http://www.hani.co.kr/arti/english_edition/e_national/611326.html
[8] http://www.huffingtonpost.com/2014/02/05/thomas-monson-fraud_n_4733418.html
[9] http://www.lfpress.com/2013/12/20/federal-government-spent-50-million-on-ontario-community-projects
[10] http://www.lfpress.com/2013/09/06/londons-unemployment-rate-dropped-in-august
[11] http://content.usatoday.com/communities/Religion/post/2012/06/fred-luter-elected-southern-baptist-first-black-president/1#.UrWop7N3vIU

[12] http://www.telegraph.co.uk/news/uknews/1492271/Sentamu-becomes-Britains-first-black-archbishop.html

[13] http://www.gmanetwork.com/news/story/302895/news/nation/catholic-groups-to-endorse-6-to-8-candidates-in-2013-polls

[14] http://sg.news.yahoo.com/millions-attend-gathering-powerful-philippine-sect-100410587.html

[15] http://www.cnn.com/2010/US/01/13/haiti.pat.robertson/

[16] http://www.tulsaworld.com/archives/oral-roberts-opens-city-of-faith-center/article_39439e18-3a1f-55a3-9d7c-54f5c67a92a9.html

[17] http://content.time.com/time/nation/article/0,8599,1677098,00.html

[18] http://www.lds.org/scriptures/dc-testament/od/1

[19] http://en.wikipedia.org/wiki/Medieval_Inquisition

[20] http://en.wikipedia.org/wiki/Spanish_Inquisition

[21] http://www.huffingtonpost.com/2014/02/05/un-report-denounces-vatican_n_4728975.html?ir=Religion&utm_campaign=020514&utm_medium=email&utm_source=Alert-religion&utm_content=FullStory

[22] Bart D. Ehrman, *Misquoting Jesus: The Story Behind Who Changed the Bible and Why* (USA: Harper Collins, 2005), p. 90.

[23] http://en.wikipedia.org/wiki/Biblical_canon

[24] http://www.ecanadanow.com/canada/2014/02/06/cana

dian-astrophysicist-says-more-more-life-hospitable-planets-than-previously-imagined/

[25] http://www.nasa.gov/ames/kepler/nasas-kepler-mission-announces-a-planet-bonanza/#.UyH3AvldVo

[26] http://www.theguardian.com/world/2014/jan/17/hiroo-onoda-japanese-soldier-dies

[27] Check http://www.talkorigins.org/faqs/flood-myths.html

[28] http://www.huffingtonpost.com/2014/02/06/carbon-dated-camel-bones-bible_n_4737437.htm

[29] Ibid.

[30] http://religion.blogs.cnn.com/2012/10/09/survey-one-in-five-americans-is-religiously-unaffiliated/

[31] http://www.huffingtonpost.com/2012/08/14/atheism-rise-religiosity-decline-in-america_n_1777031.html

www.ingramcontent.com/pod-product-compliance
Lightning Source LLC
Chambersburg PA
CBHW072001150426
43194CB00008B/954